AF260780

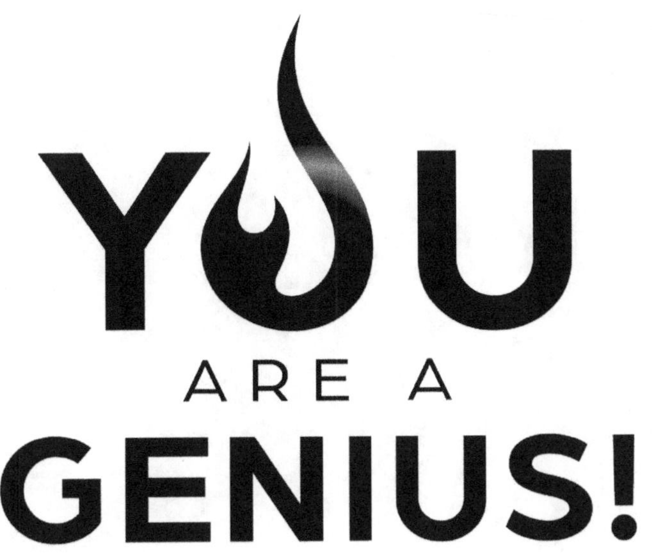

YOU
ARE A
GENIUS!

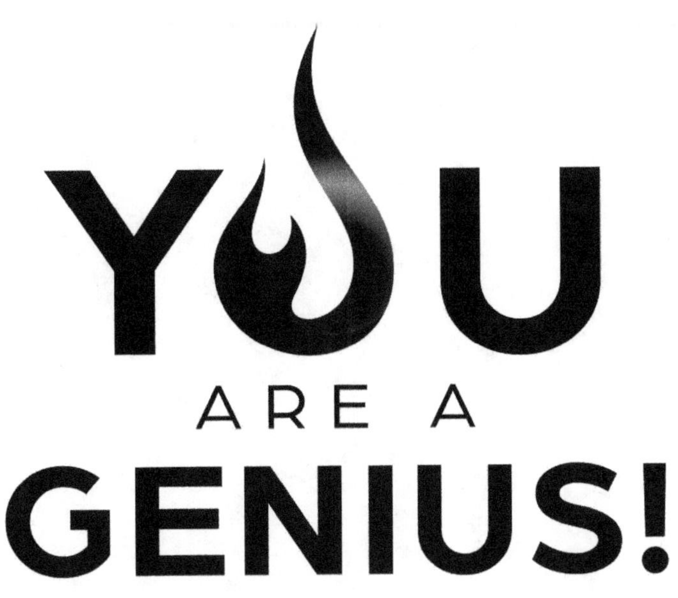

YOU
ARE A
GENIUS!

HOW TO MASTER THE
SECRETS
OF THE CREATIVE ELITE

DOC BATES

FIRST EDITION

Library of Congress Cataloging-in-Publication Data has been applied for.

ISBN 978-1-5136-4034-1

For Dawn

Contents

"Neither a lofty degree of intelligence nor imagination nor both together go to the making of genius. Love, love, love, that is the soul of genius."

— <u>Wolfgang Amadeus Mozart</u>

Preface

First of all, get excited! Because this book is going to change your life. It's going to bring you closer to your dreams. As I write these words, I reflect upon my life as a songwriter and have to ask myself what qualifies me to write a book on this subject? What makes a songwriter successful? What makes a songwriter a master? I've never had a number one hit although I'm confident I've written many songs that *could* be with the right singer at the right time. I've had cuts on the albums of a few other artists, I've personally released 6 singles as a solo recording artist. I've had one charted single with a rock band, I've heard my songs on the radio many times which is a great feeling, and I get a modest royalty check quarterly from a record which was released in 2001. On the performance side, I have toured the US multiple times over and performed for millions of people including live radio and television broadcasts. I've stood at a merchandise table and talked to an endless line of fans for hours at a time signing everything imaginable. I've experienced the fleeting euphoria of celebrity and subsequently, the enduring anonymity that often follows fame and fortune, minus the fortune....

The short answer on the other hand is... This is not really just a book about songwriting, it is a book about stimulating your creativity. I happen to be a songwriter, but the principles I discuss in this book for the most part, highlight the techniques and strategies that any creative person can use to stimulate and spark the creative genius within. So wherever I talk specifically about songwriting, just substitute whatever it is you do in place of those terms and keep reading. This is not just another book about songwriting, it is a book about creativity. It is about the why, how, when, and where you can work to maximize your creative genius.   In this book I will teach you many very specific strategies. Some of you will employ them all, some of you will only use one or two, but I guarantee you this, the use of even one of these proven strategies can accelerate your creative power into high gear. Implement them all, and you will see your creativity go into overdrive.

I met a songwriter recently who had just moved to Nashville. I asked him to play me one of his songs and he did. It was awful. Poorly conceived, poorly written, poorly performed. I smiled and asked him to play me another, he said well, that's the only one I have finished right now. I didn't have the heart to tell him that even his one song was not yet finished. I didn't want to hurt his feelings, but I wanted so badly to tell him what was wrong and how to fix it. So I encouraged him to keep it up and assured him that his songs will get better and better.

He asked me for my help, but I didn't know where to start, he simply had too far to go for me to address it in a short, chance meeting. I owe that kid a thank you because the frustration I felt at that moment led to something wonderful. That's when I sat down and started writing this book. In this book, You will learn how to generate endless ideas and create a multitude of songs. You will be given all the tools you need to take your songwriting/creativity to the next level.   You will learn to leverage your desire for success against the lifetime of knowledge and experience at my disposal. Someone once said, "give me the right lever and I can move the world." This book is that creative leverage you need to use in order to move your world and bend it to your will.

A little more about me… I started writing songs when I was 10 years old, and never stopped. I have over 38 years in the craft. I did some undergraduate work right out of high school at Southern Arkansas University before joining the Army, then later spent a few years in sales before going into the music business full time in my mid 20's. I then spent the next 10 years or so as a recording artist doing all the things a recording artist does until a life-altering injury sidelined me. As I was lying In the hospital in agony after surgery to repair a severely injured back, I had time to reflect on how I wanted to spend the rest of my life. I had young children who were facing growing up without me around… something had to give. I decided I wanted to do something in healthcare, so I returned to my studies at Rockhurst University in Kansas City and earned a BA in Psychology and a Master of Occupational Therapy. Throughout all that time at University as a full-time student, I opened and ran my own music school full time and have continued to teach over these past years while practicing therapy. After 10 years in therapy, a lifetime of teaching, performing and composing music, all of my background has now converged and demands to be shared with you.

The great thing about being a human *and* doing what we are meant to do is that it makes us happy, it promotes a feeling of well-being that you cannot get in any other way. You've probably heard the term "happy as a pig in mud." Why is the pig happy? Because he is doing what he is meant to do, he is in his element. He is content. This is where you need to be as a creative genius. This is your "happy place." The problem with creativity is, most creative people are not fully aware of their power or of their potential and therefore wind up living well below that potential. As a result they may well be that pig in mud, but they are not up to their necks in it, but rather, that mud is barely squishing up between their toes. I hope that everyone who reads this book will eventually find themselves up to their necks.

Whether you are a painter, a baker, a salesman, writer, entrepreneur, singer, student or wannabe of any variety, this book is for you. It is about promoting the happiest possible version of you by finding and unlocking your personal mud bath. All the mud you could ever want to wallow in is already inside you and I'm going to help you bring it out if you will only allow it. As an added bonus, you are going to understand the true meaning of contentment and spread that happiness to everyone within your sphere of influence. You are going to become a better you through the power of your own creative genius. At times, this book will seem like a success manual, although this is not entirely intentional, you really cannot achieve success in what you do without resulting in a greater level of happiness. It is simply not possible to address the output of the creative genius without acknowledging the happiness that will inevitably result.

I give a lot of examples throughout this book and talk about other artists and songwriters and creative people whom I've know over the years, but to protect the guilty, I won't use names on the embarrassing stuff. I use examples of what *not* to do occasionally because I believe in learning from our own mistakes as well as the mistakes of others. Mistakes can be a powerful professor. Ignore the lessons your mistakes have to offer and you are doomed to repeat them until you do. I am a generally positive person, so I don't wish to dwell on the negative stuff, mostly I share with you only those experiences which I believe will benefit you on some level. I will not be guilty of gossiping about other writers or artists, so please don't ask me to.

You can guess who these people might be if you want, but I choose to protect their anonymity since I'll probably be writing about their bad habits. We want to learn what we can from our mentors through both the dos and the don'ts they can teach us. It is important to make this distinction as, from my observation, even the most perfect and the most successful people are every bit as flawed as you and me. I don't have to be perfect to teach you, just as those whom I've learned the most from also taught me that perfection can never be truly attained, and no matter how successful we are in life and in our chosen fields - no matter what level of financial or critical success we attain, we are all just people trying to be better people, or at the least… Better at what we do. And if we weren't flawed in the first place, how could we ever learn? What would we have to gain by trying?

That being said, someone smarter than me once said the following, and somehow I remembered it... "When you teach someone else, you get to learn it twice." I write this because you may be one of those people who tells him/herself, "I don't know enough to teach." Well let me learn you something right now... Everyone knows something, and anyone can teach what they know. Find a student to pass along your knowledge to. Find someone you can mentor and thereby perpetuate the circle of learning. It will enrich your life in many ways.

Of all the things I've done in the music business, I consider my most enduring, rewarding, and ultimately, important achievement to be personified in the scores of students I have instructed on the creation and performance of music. I absolutely love teaching and I consider it such an honor to have contributed to the development of so many wonderful young adults. I have had the privilege of instructing kids who have gone on to become successful recording artists, songwriters, teachers, engineers, producers and performers. That is what this book is about for me. Taking teaching to the next level. I've already proven that my methods produce successful music industry professionals. Now I feel a moral obligation to pass on my knowledge and experience to you. I can't wait to see what you do with it. Hit me up on facebook or instagram and let me know what your experiences have been with these techniques. Join the creative collective and let's all share and grow together. I sincerely appreciate your feedback as it makes me a better educator. Fair warning though, if you share with me, you may find your insights being regurgitated in my next book.

My real world experience as a writer and entertainer; educational background in psychology and clinical background as a registered and licensed occupational therapist give me a unique perspective on the science of creativity and how it applies to your goals and dreams. Through greater understanding of the human body and specifically the brain as it relates to creativity, this book will provide an edge that you will use to punch through your personal barriers to achieve your fullest potential.

I understand why people in Nashville welcome outsiders, but are hesitant to work with them until they "make the move." Moving to Nashville is seen as an "act of faith." By professionals in the music industry and for good reason.   If you want to be a successful songwriter, I suggest that you move there. There is no better place to ply your trade than Nashville, but keep in mind that it is not an absolute necessity and that wherever you are, there are people in your community who are interested in connecting with you toward the purpose of greater creativity and productivity. In short, wherever you are, there are others like you nearby. Find them and connect with other positive people who can both mentor you and be mentored by you.

So what do I know about creativity?   I just looked back through my notes on my cell phone dated this week. I counted 36 song seeds, 12 completed lyrics, and 3 songs actually finished and demos recorded and that is while working several hours a day on the book you are now reading.   I work with multiple Nashville recording artists out of my home studio in the midwest, and I put out, by anyone's standards, a staggering volume of work considering the fact that I only write part time. I have written over 28 songs in the past month, and more songs than I can count over the past several years, and there is no end in sight. So when I visit Nashville and speak with young songwriters who are struggling for every idea, I don't just shake my head in disbelief... It literally boggles my mind. So many are struggling for their next idea. This is heartbreaking to watch.   For me it's like watching someone break into their car with a brick while I stand idly by holding the key. I just want to help you kick it up a notch, if you are working hard, you deserve it.

Why do ideas and lyrics flow from me like water while much of the industry seems to flounder in a desert, desperate for an original idea? Because they don't know what veteran songwriters know, and as far as I can tell, no one else is teaching the system the way that this book does. If you implement the same strategies as successful people, you will be successful, it's that simple. I am here to train you to train yourself to use the same techniques that many professional creatives have used for hundreds of years to stimulate and perpetuate the creative genius within. There is no reason why you can't be just as successful as you desire to be.

How to use this book

You will find that I will often repeat important points in this book. Whenever I read a book of my own, I like to highlight, and underline and write in the margins and such. You may be reading this as an E-book or on a device like a tablet or computer, which limits your ability to make notes, unless you want to mark up your computer screen, which I don't recommend. So, I have set apart and highlighted the points that I believe are key in importance and impact, they are set apart from the main text.

Once you have finished this book for the first time, I suggest you pick it up and give it a re-read every day for the next 30 days or so. This is easier than it sounds as you will just be skimming through and stopping only to read the highlighted portions and subsets. By doing this, you will reinforce the good habits and remind your subconscious mind of what the book is about and which parts are the most important to you. Furthermore, as you implement strategies and you see them work in your life, you will want to continue to add more of them as you go along. There will be many strategies you wish to implement, but trying them all at once would be a daunting challenge. So just implement them one or two at a time and add to them as you go. Later on there will be a chapter that goes through a "day in the life." Where I will reveal many of the strategies which I employ daily and which work for me. All of these strategies may not be for you…. Just implement the ones that seem to help you the most. I believe that as you gain experience and success with a few of them, you will get excited about adding more. Once you begin to implement these strategies, you will see your creative genius explode.

Throughout this book I will refer to the "creative genius." Whenever I use this term, I am talking about you. I want you to begin to refer to yourself as the creative genius in your thoughts. A genius is defined as a person with exceptional creative power, and that is exactly what you are if you are a writer, painter, sculptor, entrepreneur, or etcetera… Not just anyone can create art, that makes you exceptional and by definition, a genius. If the term sounds more grandiose than you feel, then enjoy the promotion, you deserve it and you didn't even know it.

"But Doc, I don't *feel* like a genius." As I said earlier, you will *feel* happy and complete only when you are *doing* what you are meant to do. This concept is not necessarily about what you feel, it's more about what you do. In other words, if you choose to *do* all the right things, the *feelings* will follow. "But Doc, I'm not yet worthy to be called a genius." **Not True!** You are what you allow yourself to become. This is not wishful thinking, it is not believing for a miracle, it is not lying to yourself. This is the essence of metacognition at work. You are what you think you are, so be careful what you call yourself, because you may actually be foolish enough to believe what you say… most of us are. Sticks and stones may break your bones, but words and yes, even thoughts can do far more damage to you and your life, your well-being, your motivation, your creativity, and your work product. Get out a piece of paper, write those lies onto it in bold letters then rip it up into pieces, wad it into the ball of garbage that it is, and toss it in the trash where it belongs. Or better yet…

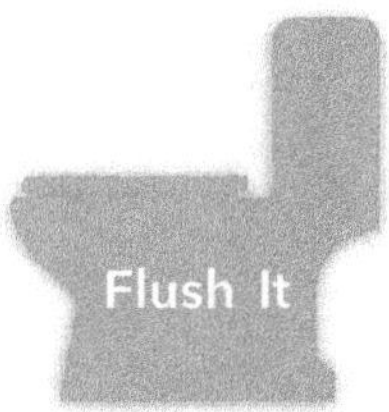

To *create* you must *do*, to *do* you must first *imagine*. And the imagination is the single most powerful tool you have at your disposal. Listen and I will help you learn to use it to greater effect. When I was a kid, I imagined a day when I would carry a powerful computer around in my pocket, live in a great big house, drive an exotic car, marry a beautiful woman and have smart and successful children. I dreamed I would write beautiful songs, sing in front of millions of people, hear my songs on the radio, author books, speak before other professionals and teach the masses. My dreams just keep coming true in spades, and so can yours, but you have to dare to imagine it all first. I have more dreams, many more and they just keep growing and getting bigger and bolder.

You are the sum total of your thoughts, your experiences and your actions. And your work product is a direct reflection of who you are. An apple tree grows apples, a peach tree grows peaches… Ask yourself… what am I growing? What do I want to grow? If you are reading this book, you have a desire to become that creative genius that you need to be in order to maximize your potential. Get it through your head, get it through your heart. Say it out loud and live it! Touch your heart and repeat after me now and every day…

I am a creative genius

First, make yourself a reputation for being a creative genius. Second, surround yourself with partners who are better than you are. Third, leave them to go get on with it.

-<u>David Ogilvy</u>

Secret #1

Seek Creative Flow

The intention of this book is to teach you the **secret methods** of successful creatives. A recent trip to Nashville got me to thinking… *maybe I can help teach other songwriters what I know and have some fun while doing it.* I was right, I have enjoyed organizing and presenting this subject more than anything I've done in a very long time. At this point in my life I truly want to inspire the next generation. You can reach your fullest potential with just a bit of a push in the right direction. With a bit of help, young creatives can live up to their potential, if you are a veteran, you can still kick it up into high gear. It is my most sincere hope that you take this information and move forward and be enormously successful in the music business, or the fashion business, or the widget business. All of your dreams can come true. The purpose of this book is to help you get there faster.

I know a famous songwriter who lives in Nashville who we do not want to emulate. His name is Steve. Now Steve had a major hit record with a modern-day cultural icon early in his career, and in my estimation, that success ruined his life. Although he is quite famous and revered among other songwriters, he seems miserable most of the time. Now granted, I only know for sure what I've observed in person over dozens of meetings and the scores of hours I probably wasted just hanging out with him because I was in awe of his success. I'm a pretty good observer, and Steve was a real piece of work. I am going to dissect his habits throughout this book as an example of what *not* to do. When I refer to success, I'm really talking about happiness and purpose-driven success, not money and fame-driven success. I've seen both kinds up close, and the latter is ugly, fleeting, and empty without the former. Please take a moment to truly understand this.

Now when I refer to Steve's "success" I mean my 25 year-old former self's "idea" of what success should look like. You know, the usual... cars, money, fancy houses, a life of leisure, etc... Now that I'm older and wiser, I know better. Don't get me wrong... I mean I have all that stuff now, plenty of money, fancy car, fancy house, beautiful wife etc... But I'm also truly happy because my life has purpose. I don't think Steve's life truly had purpose back then, I truly hope he's turned things around. But for our purposes, Steve will represent the pitfalls we wish to avoid to be truly successful. So, do not be a Steve!

The most talented people I have ever met, and there have been many, were among the most humble. Visit Nashville and you will find yourself surrounded by them but you'll never know it. They aren't flashy or arrogant for the most part, they are simply locked into a groove of creativity that flows and they nurture that creativity daily. As you read on, define what your flow should look like to you. It's okay to want to better yourself, level up your home and your car if that's what you are in to. There's nothing wrong with wanting "stuff." But when you make it your main focus, it is self-defeating because even if you get it all tomorrow you will be left with an empty feeling without the purpose-driven happiness we all ultimately desire… whether we know it or not. So no matter what happens, stay in your groove and keep your creative habits in a constant state of flow.

Fortune has rarely condescended to be the companion of genius.

<u>-Isaac D'Israeli</u>

Secret #2

Don't Wait For Inspiration

I've been teaching music and songwriting for 30 years, and the most common question I get is, "Where does your inspiration come from?" To be successful, you need to be able to get inspired and stay inspired with a very minimal amount of effort and no interruption of your creative flow. Quite simply, if you follow my instructions, you will never get writer's block again. Your creativity will soar to new heights and depths. Your creative ideas will pour forth like an endless fount. I will answer the question above once and for all, and then I will proceed to explain how inspiration works and where it comes from throughout the rest of this book. My answer has been the same for the last 20 years or so.

Inspiration is for amateurs

I will explain… Only amateurs sit around waiting for inspiration to strike **before** creation begins. The creative genius does not wait for inspiration… he creates with passion, purpose and discipline knowing that real creativity will only follow his effort. The creative genius does not need to be inspired in order to **begin** the process. He is inspired

by the process *as* it unfolds. If you are waiting for inspiration, you are killing your creativity and wasting precious time as you do so.

Remember Steve? He would often do this. Steve had a handful of big hits with major artists, but for the most part, he did a whole lot of nothing, he did it everyday, and he took a lot of naps while doing it. He was not a "sit down and work" guy. He was a sit around and "wait for inspiration to strike like lightening" guy. He never said so, but Steve "lived" writer's block. He just seemed to meander through life with no drive or purpose and a completely undisciplined approach bordering on disrespect of the creative process as I have come to understand it. Steve was a professional songwriter who behaved like an amateur. He was not the exception to the rule. It is important as we take this journey together to remember that Steve is unhappy and lives a depressing life, most likely because he isn't doing anything meaningful with it. Don't be a Steve.

I have been around songwriters all my life and if I've heard it once I've heard it a zillion times. "I have writer's block." If you have suffered from what is commonly known as writer's block, you are not alone. Millions of writers of all ages, disciplines, genres and skill level have feared this terrible malady for millennia. It is the single most dreaded disease a writer can contract, and yet is the most misunderstood of all. Simply by understanding the creative process, you can easily overcome this fictitious and mysterious disease known as *writer's block* and never suffer again.

The most important thing to remember about writer's block is this… it does not truly exist. There is nothing magical about the ability to create. It is an innate process that humans have been engaged in since the dawn of man. By throwing out terms like "writer's block," we take the process out of our own hands and place it under the spell of nebulous forces which we cannot hope to control.   Once the responsibility for creativity has been shifted from the writer's control, he can then rest easy and do nothing for as long as it takes him to get inspired again.

It is important for the creative genius to understand that the ability to create is not based on some outside force which is out of your control. The ability to create is 100% within your power and influence. If you are not able to create, there is no one to blame but you, and the sooner you realize this and accept the responsibility for your creativity, the sooner you can begin to understand the many ways in which you can guide your own creativity to new heights and beyond.

Sorry if this gets a little harsh, but I'm going to give you some tough love here, after which I promise… If you stay with me, I will help you overcome all obstacles to your creativity and help you place the helm of your ship firmly back under your control where it belongs. So, here goes…. Writer's block is an excuse lazy people use to get out of work. I call it "writer's excuse."

Let me make one distinction. Writer's block is not clinical depression. If you have clinical depression, it can stifle your creativity, but that is not what we are talking about. The issue here is not one of mental health, the present issue is the fear of the blank page. The blank page can do you no harm. It cannot hurt you and poses no threat to your person or your family. The blank page is your friend, not your enemy. Every blank page has a song already written on it, your job is to add the ink. Make an affirmation to yourself right now. Place your hand over your heart and say it with me out loud:

The Blank Page Is My Friend

Throughout this book, I will ask you to make some affirmations which are designed to help reprogram your flawed thinking about your skills and talents. It is important that you say them aloud so that you are reading, speaking, hearing, and touching yourself throughout this experience. Engage all of your senses in this learning process and you will get much more out of it. At the end of this book you will find a page full of affirmations that you should download and print and place somewhere in your home where you can see and perform them daily. This will cement the learning that will take place throughout this book and increase the likelihood that you will carry forward what you will have learned here. If you really want to overcome your personal demons and release the floodgates of your creativity, it will require something of you. It is a process and I encourage you to let it happen.

Responsibility is one of the keys to understanding the creative process. There is nothing necessarily magical or spiritual about writing. The reason I make this distinction early in this book is because there are millions of writers out there who constantly attribute their success or failure to a third party, be it a god or a muse, or some whim of fate. If you cannot take responsibility for your own creativity, you will never be a professional writer. That is why I say inspiration is for amateurs. I tell all my students this because it is so very true and so very often misunderstood.

To clarify, I will give you an example: Imagine that you need to buy a birthday cake. So, you go into the grocery store and amble over to the bakery, belly up to the counter, smile and say, "excuse me sir, I would like to buy a cake today." Now, the bakery manager looks across to you, bows his head solemnly and with a tear in his eye sniffs and says… "I'm sorry sir but I'm just not feeling it today. I'm pretty sure I've got *bakers block.*"

If your baker, banker, butcher, waitress, builder or lawyer had to wait for inspiration to strike before going to work, you would replace them immediately, but often as writers, we have this vague, sketchy and suspect diagnosis we can self ascribe to our failure to do our jobs.

Suppose you went to drop your toddler off at daycare and you found a sign on the door which said, "For creative reasons, we must take a personal day to reflect." I think we can all agree this is a ridiculous way to do business and you would never tolerate it. You would fire any professional in your life who behaved this way so go ahead and fire yourself. Fire your undertrained, misguided, flawed self, and give the job instead to the new you. The better informed, prepared you. The you who is the creative genius. The first step is to admit you have a problem, the second is to understand the solution. If I am describing you, take heart, because you're about to solve a major problem in your life. Read on… You have got this!

If you are a writer, you have to find a way to do your job with the same level of consistency and reliability that you would demand of any other professional. Otherwise, you are a hypocrite of the highest order. This book is designed to help you to identify what is holding you back and kickstart yourself into action in each and every moment you live.

Writer's block does not truly exist

Get it out of your head, out of your vocabulary and out of your life. It is nothing more than negative energy designed to provide the slovenly writer the *out* he so desperately desires. If you do not want to write, then just don't write. Just say you're taking a day or week or year off, say you only write when you feel like it. But please… Don't go around telling people you have writer's block like it's some kind of incurable disease.   There's no such thing… Touch your chest and say this affirmation with me.

I take full responsibility for my own creativity or lack thereof

There is no outside force that will make you more or less able to write. You are in control, you are at the helm of your own ship, and you get to decide where the rudder turns and where the bow points. You are powerful and capable… Get it through your head. Touch your heart and say it out loud and just try and suppress the grin that appears…

I am a creative genius

"So Doc, I believe you, there's no such thing as writer's block, now what?" I'm glad you asked reader and friend… Now we can get down to business and start creating.   What every writer needs is an endless and boundless supply of ideas and up until now, you have struggled, scrimped and saved your whole life like every idea is going to be your last. I've been in and around the Nashville scene for 30 years, and I've seen this among even the most elite of songwriters. I've been to a writing session where everyone looks at me and says, "the new guy has

to bring the idea." If anyone says that to me now, I can literally throw ideas at them for hours and never run out. Oftentimes, other writers are astonished at how many ideas I am prepared to offer.

I refer to ideas as *song seeds*. Song seeds are the beginning of every song you create. A song seed is what every song grows from. It could be a single word, a title idea, or a melodic idea or hook. It can actually just be an idea for a story that your song will tell. I love to write songs which start with a story, and often when I hear of a compelling story from a friend or on television or a movie, I will sketch the basic story and attempt to write a song based on it. I recently saw a movie about a teenaged girl who is desperately trying to find her way in life. I sketched the idea out briefly and put it in my seed silo. As a creative genius, you should analyze every piece of life that comes at you and extract the story from it. Those seeds will germinate and slowly grow sometimes for weeks, months or years before the completed song emerges.

Remember Steve? He never seemed to have a list of ideas to work from, about once a month or so, he might pull one out of thin air and write a song, but the majority of his songs, and I've heard most of them… were not all that good. Let me clarify, Steve is a fairly intelligent guy, but while his songs were well crafted, catchy and clever, they were also based, for the most part… on bad ideas. I often told Steve, "you are a songwriter's songwriter," which was both a compliment and a hard truth at the same time.   Here's why… Other songwriters recognized the depth and cleverness of his writing whereas the average person would never appreciate it, and the vast majority of the songs lacked any real commercial quality or appeal because the ideas were dated and flawed. I mean these ideas were the sort of ideas that would never make it out of my *seed silo*, which I will discuss in greater detail later.

Don't be like Steve with an anorexic idea backlog, always struggling to find the next bit of inspiration. Steve was able to take a bad idea and write an amazingly clever lyric with virtually no mass market appeal. Imagine what he could've accomplished with an endless supply of great ideas? Be an endless source of material. There is an infinite amount of songs waiting to be written. Think of a grain silo where a farmer keeps his seeds. How numerous are those seeds? Aspire and expect for your seeds to pile up in innumerable quantity, and they will.

His genius he was quite content in one
brief sentence to define; Of inspiration one
percent, of perspiration, ninety nine.
<u>Thomas A. Edison</u>

Secret # 3

Create Abundance

I've sat in a meeting with veteran songwriters with number one hits to their credits who were still so stingy with their ideas that they are literally holding back their best in songwriting sessions. "This is your job!" I thought. "You should be guiding me, not the other way around." Here is one of the greatest secrets I know which holds even the greatest creatives back every single day. Stinginess breeds scarcity while generosity breeds abundance.

Stinginess breeds scarcity

If you are one of these people who goes around hoarding your own ideas, afraid to share them openly and unreservedly, you are literally manufacturing a false scarcity, and when you do this, the price shoots up. Where fear rules, faith fails. You have to change your way of thinking here. Most creative people treat ideas as if they are few and far between, as if they are scarce, as if they are finite in quantity. Nothing could possibly be farther from the truth. Say it with me...

I create my own scarcity or abundance

For example, imagine there is a farmer who wants to plant a crop of corn, so he goes to the seed merchant and says, "I need enough seeds to plant a hundred acres." So the dealer says, "Sir, haven't you heard, seeds are hard to come by these days. It seems we sold so many the last few years that there are hardly any left… in fact, the more that get planted, the less there are to sell. So, I'm only going to be able to sell you a few this year, here you go…" The farmer walks away from this exchange holding a fraction of the amount of seeds he needs to be productive and a very real fear for the well-being of his farm and family. Because of his fear, he is terrified to part with what few seeds he has, and instead hordes them as if they are the last seeds he may ever see. He is so freaked out that he is actually afraid to do the one thing that would solve all his problems… plant them.

In this example, it is important to note that, first of all there is no real shortage of seeds. The logic of the seed merchant is flawed, and he passes his flawed logic and baseless and illogical fear onto the farmer who then is very likely to spread the fear to his family, friends, neighbors and colleagues. Imagine that he goes back to his farm and says to his neighbor, "Haven't you heard about the seed shortage? Seeds are hard to come by, so we'll be lucky to even get a crop put in this year. My family will probably lose the farm." His neighbors lament his bad luck and assume there's will be the same. This false sense of scarcity may actually have now blossomed into a full blown crop failure for the entire community. Unfortunately it is ridiculous.

On the surface, the logic of the seed merchant makes sense, but in actuality he is utterly and completely wrong. Planting more seeds will produce exponentially more seeds, it will never use them up. It is impossible for the farmer in this example to use up all the seeds unless he has forgotten how to farm altogether. In actuality, the more seeds he plants, the more he will harvest and so on. It is the same with song seeds. We have ten thousand songwriters running around Nashville fearing a crop failure that continues to come year after year because they themselves have created it with their negativity through the **power of expectation**. We often get what we truly expect in life and this is a prime example. If you want to turn it around, realize that the more seeds you plant the more you will harvest, and furthermore, it would be unreasonable **not** to expect that harvest.

The law of sewing and reaping… literally every traditional wisdom and school of thought teaches this principle, and yet as creative people, we tend to ignore all of that wisdom and say, "it doesn't apply to me." Well I am here to tell you… you are sorely mistaken! If this is your thinking, what a wonderful gift you now have been given. Now you can let go of all the worry and expect the harvest you deserve. This principle applies to you as much in creativity as in any other area of life, love or finances. This is a universal principle. This is the *law* of sowing and reaping, and whether you subscribe to a religious doctrine or not, this law is as absolute as the law of gravity. Try to defy it, and you will fail. If you plant one apple seed, it grows into a tree which produces an infinite amount of apples for as long as it lives. This law works whether you want it to or not… that's why it's called a *law*. If your life is an endless chain of negativity, chaos, and calamity, you need to identify those seeds and stop planting them. If your life is full of positivity, optimism, and plenty, again, this is a direct result of the seeds you have planted. Find more of the positive seeds and keep planting them daily. Throughout this book, I will be providing you with affirmations which are designed to "kickstart" your positivity, your creativity, and assist you to begin to create habits which will plant the kinds of seeds in your life that are essential to the creative genius.

Now that you understand the law of sewing and reaping, re-read my "parable of the seed merchant" keeping the following explanation in mind and try and wrap your head around just how ridiculous it is. Your inner voice (the seed merchant) tells you that ideas (seeds) are scarce. It convinces you that if you use too many ideas (seeds) on one song you might not have enough for the next one. It convinces you that your ideas aren't good enough. If convinces you that your ideas aren't as good as your co-writer's ideas. It convinces you that you should keep your ideas (seeds) to yourself and that you should never share them (plant a crop) with your co-writers. You essentially expect this poor harvest, and yet you are surprised when you get it, curse your luck, and damn your circumstances and stunted intellect. Poor you… Can't you see you get what you give. It's all quite simple… give more - get more.

Remember Steve? I don't believe he ever understood this concept, and as a result he had very few ideas and very few songs. What we all want and need in order to be successful, is an abundance of ideas. The more the better. And only when you have a thousand ideas to choose from in a writing session do your songs begin to elevate to the one in a million level. If this is the level you want to live with, build your seed

To write a one-in-a-million song…
first endeavor to write a million

bank constantly. I will continue to expand on this concept and discuss it as we go along. If you want to write a one-in-a-million song, it's quite simple… first write a million songs, or at the very least, collect a million ideas.

What you need to understand right now is that your mind is a wellspring of ideas. You do not have a limit. You are not going to awaken one day and find that the well has run dry. It will never ever happen, period! The faster you can change this obstructive attitude, the faster your brain will start handing out the ideas like halloween candy. You see, your subconscious is the gate keeper and the liar who constantly tells you. *Whoa, don't share that here, you may never get another idea that good. Keep that to yourself or someone will steal it.* If you are like most writers, like a fool, you are listening to every word your negative brain says. When your brain tells you this lie, say to yourself, "My mind is an endless wellspring of ideas, the more I produce, the more will come." I like to think of my brain as bursting with ideas such that they are literally pushing their way out. In fact, say it with me as you touch your heart…

**My every idea has ten more
behind it pushing it out**

What does this mean? Well in short, it means that the more ideas you generate, the more ideas you will generate. It is not the ideas themselves that are scarce, it is your flawed programming that fabricates this scarcity. Fortunately, all you have to do to reverse this process and thereby open the floodgates of ideas is to convince your constipated intellect that there is no danger. There is no reason to fear that the ideas will stop, and there is therefore no reason to hoard the ideas. To do this, you have to be mindful of your thoughts. I will get more into this concept in a later chapter where we will discuss in detail the magic of reprogramming your brain. In the meantime, use these above affirmations to begin to reprogram your flawed ways of thinking.

I can relate to the feeling of panic when you need to be working on music but can't seem to generate a decent idea.   I just don't feel it anymore. Early in my career, I was terrified of not having ideas and what few ideas I got were less than stellar. I hung out with other writers who all seemed to be constantly at odds with the idea generator. There was a certain writer, with whom I had an appointment early one morning to write. His name was Kenny Beard, and this single writing session changed my life. What a magnanimous and generous human being Kenny was that day. I didn't realize it, but he had blocked off the entire day to just hang out with me. When I showed up to the session, I had no idea what to expect. I mean, this guy had something like fifty charted hits and a dozen number ones to his credit and I felt the pressure to produce.

So I showed up to the session and busted out my best ideas from my idea notebook, and he just shrugged his shoulders and said nah, let's just hang out and visit, we'll come up with something good. This guy had absolutely no anxiety about coming up with ideas. He had faith that the ideas would come and he was completely relaxed about it. I had been writing with all these uptight guys who had been offloading their anxiety onto me. I had been led to believe that great ideas were like a vein of gold, or worse like Sasquatch in that, they are so rare that you may write your whole life and never actually have a great idea like the ones we hear on the radio. What Kenny taught me that day was this… *ideas are everywhere, all around us all the time and constantly available*… we just have to pay attention. Ideas are literally *life* coming at you all day every day. If you are alive… you are surrounded by them.

Nowadays, I can sit down and just start writing. I'm producing song after song after song, and they just keep on coming. Within a few minutes of sitting down to work I'm onto something good. I don't struggle anymore. When it's time to write, I just sit down and do it. I have an enormous backlog of ideas and get new ones almost everyday. Several times a week, I may write three or four complete lyrics in one day. My biggest problem is producing demos. I like to do it myself, but I have literally a hundred or more songs just waiting to be demo'd. I can't keep up. It's a good problem to have. Yes I'd like to have all that work caught up, yes I'd like to have the kind of hit record that would give me the freedom to stop everything else and catch up, but if that never happens, its truly okay because I'm truly happy doing what I'm doing. I'm a pig in mud, and I'm up to my ears in it because I am creating and I'm helping others. This is what I was truly meant to do. This is clearly my purpose and I feel so very lucky to have found it.

More importantly for the reader of this book to know is, I have multiple students who produce just as well or, in many cases, better than I do. I have one kid who I taught for over ten years who goes into his studio every single day and leaves at the end of the day with as many as three or four songs *done*. I said done! I'm talking about concept to demo in one session, multiple songs every day of the week. This is remarkable. At this rate, this kid could literally produce an album a week and I've seen him do it over and over again. This is not magic, this is training, talent, and skill all converging to form a staggering body of work. The cool thing is, if I can teach him to do it, I can teach you to do it. You just have to put the time in. Remember, this kid I'm talking about is 18 years old, but he's been working at it for just over 10 years and he is already approaching a level of mastery that most of us don't reach till we're 30 or so.

Where will you be in 10 years? Whether you plan on being in the music business or whatever your creative business is, you may as well be great at it. You may as well be excellent. Don't be afraid of the work or the time as long as the ride is enjoyable. If a task looks so daunting that it makes you consider quitting, you are looking at it the wrong way. Instead of thinking to yourself, "Gosh I don't have 10 years to spare to spend elevating my skill level." Instead, think to yourself, "Gosh, I can't imagine doing anything else with my life for the next 10 years." In 10 years you will be *somewhere* doing *something*. It will either be something you love that inspires you and gives your life meaning, or it will be something you settled for like most of the drones out there. If in 10 years you find yourself in a boring, mind-numbing job, churning out widgets in some hell-hole, praying for each weekend to come faster as your life ebbs toward retirement just so you can get a break from the terrible monotony of it all, it will have occurred that way as a direct result of the decisions you make right now. And *'right now'* occurs every moment of every day for the rest of your life.

Always, *always* make the right decision *right now*. Imagine who you will be in 10 years then imagine how much fun it's going to be getting there. What you will be doing then will come only as a direct result of what you first imagine yourself doing, then systematically work toward creating. I can't stress enough just how imperative it is that you enjoy every moment of your life on some level. That's what makes the next 10 years of preparation not just bearable, but far more preferable than doing nothing inspiring. We will explore some of these concepts in greater detail in later chapters. The take home here is this…

> ## It ain't the difficulty of the work or the time required… it's the joy of the ride that matters most…

I know that the twelve notes in each octave and the variety of rhythm offer me opportunities that all of human genius will never exhaust.

-Igor Stravinsky

Secret #4

Cream Rises

Let's take a quick look back at Steve's life. Early in my career, I idolized Steve because he had co-written this iconic song which later led to a handful of other respectable hits before his light sort of waned so to speak. To my knowledge, he basically spent the next 20 years or so struggling with his former success as he saw it. Steve's major problem wasn't a lack of success in his career, it was merely in the way that he measured that success. Because he measured it by top 10 hits, he didn't have much success, and spent most of his career chasing that impossible standard. Now at the time I was hanging out a lot with Steve, he had a catalog of maybe a hundred or so songs which I thought was unbelievable. I mean I was in awe of that body of work. Wow! Now I look back and I think, geez that was nothing…. I have an 18 year old student who has a catalog of over 300 songs. But you may be saying to yourself, "Doc, isn't quality more important than quantity?" Well, I would have to say with respect… no. The quality is *within* the quantity.

The quality is within the quantity

Let me give you an example… A common phrase you hear all over Nashville is this… "The cream rises to the top." This is an analogy based on the dairy business, so I apologize if you are lactose intolerant, but it literally means this… If you have a container of milk, the cream, 'or the best' part of the milk will literally rise and float on the surface assuming your milk has not been homogenized. Figuratively, this means that the best songs, artists, producers, etcetera will, in the same manner, rise to the tops of their respective fields. The problem with this analogy is that in the music business and specifically the songwriting business, you are not merely judged by the amount of cream you have, but rather, by the size of the vat of milk you have produced. The wisdom being, the more milk, the more cream, which is both literally and figuratively true. To the songwriter, it means if your body of work consists of 20 songs (your vat of milk), you will probably have 1 keeper in the bunch (your cream). It also means that if your vat consists of 1000 songs, not only is it assumed that you have at least 200 keepers, but the further assumption is, that if you have written that many songs, your skill level is such that probably a much higher percentage of them are "cream." If your vat consists of 2000 songs, it may even be further assumed that you can sit down and write at will and the majority of your material will be solidly written and of high quality.

Using Steve as an example, his small handful of three or four hits was directly in line with his volume of work as I saw it. Maybe a hundred or so songs of questionable quality but undeniable craftsmanship. So follow me here, if 100 songs (Steve's Vat of milk) produced Steve 3 or 4 hits (Steve's cream), just imagine how many hit songs he may have had with a catalogue of 1000 songs? Later, I will discuss the difference between craftsmanship and creativity in detail… so stay tuned. If Steve were disciplined enough to rise and write just one song a day, he would have written that thousand songs in just under four years instead of carousing about Nashville cursing his rotten luck.

<u>**Tying It All Together**</u>

In this life, no matter what you are doing with yourself, you have to figure out how your success will be measured. Ultimately, you are not on this earth to please other people or to be judged by others. You are responsible only for yourself and those people who depend upon you. If your only criteria for success is to have a number one hit, that's great and I hope you achieve it. Personally, I don't measure my success in that way because if I do, I may write ten thousand songs in my career and still not consider myself a success, and that would be tragic. For me, success is in the creation, not in the reward. I have a good income and everything I need, so big time commercial success is ancillary. It would be nice, but it will never complete me. Make no mistake about it, I sincerely *desire* that commercial success the same as everyone else, but I don't *need* it. All I really need is to create value and mentor others to do the same.

Whatever it is you aspire to achieve, remember this... if you're not good enough without it, you will never be good enough with it. Align your self-worth with creation rather than reward. If you do not believe in yourself without a hit record, you will not believe in yourself after you have one. If you are trying to achieve because you expect to feel differently after you get some recognition or reward, I've got news for you. You will still be the same insecure person after you achieve whatever that *"thing"* is, which you think is going to change everything for you. Trust me on this... success won't change who you really are.

Look at it like this... what if you were granted one wish. Imagine that you are a songwriter like me and one of your songs will go to number one and stay there for 30 weeks and make you an instant millionaire and a legend in your field, but the only catch is... it's the last song you will ever write and you will never produce another. What would you do? Would you take that deal? I would take a hard pass without even thinking about it. Why? Because the joy is in the writing and that's where I measure my success. Don't get me wrong. A mega-hit song would be awesome, but if it doesn't happen it's okay. Ultimately whether I ever have a mega-hit or not, I will still wake up every day and write another song till the day I die. And I'll be happy as a pig in mud every single day. I wish the same for you my friend. May all your dreams come true in abundance. Touch your heart and say this out loud…

I owe it to myself to do what makes me happy

Genius at first is little more than a great capacity for receiving discipline.

-George Eliot

Secret # 5

Develop Skills

Brace yourself because here comes that tough love again…. Writing is a *skill* not a talent. A skill is something that you use over and over and the more you use it, the better you get at it. It is not a talent that is bestowed upon you by a third party or fate or a god.

Writing is a skill not a talent

The reason I make this distinction is that people often confuse the terms - "skill" and "talent." Talent is not a skill, and skill is not a talent. The two are mutually exclusive terms. Many people use these terms interchangeably much to the detriment of their own creativity. It is important to fully understand the difference between the two so that you do not make the common mistake of assuming that you just *don't have enough talent.*

More creative energy flows down the toilet due to this common misconception than to any other factor. I weep for the children who could've been great if they had only understood this fact. The lack of understanding of this concept is poison to the young and aspiring writer. If you assume you do not have enough talent, then again the responsibility flows from you and into the nebulous ether of chance.

Insisting that you don't have the measure of talent is just another way of saying, "It's not my fault that I'm not successful." If you want to convince yourself that you have no control over your creativity, it's easy. And you should be very careful, because you may actually believe every word you say, so watch what you tell yourself. Personally, I know I have talent, but more importantly… I have twice the skills, and I'll take skills over talent any old day.

I'll take skills over talent any old

Here's why… Talent, according to the dictionary definition is most generally understood as something that you are born with. People who are talented are often referred to as "gifted." And when it comes right down to it, no one is ever truly proud of a "gift." Consider this example… My son has one gaming system that he got for Christmas one year as a gift, and another one which he got a job and went out and earned all the money to pay for. Which one do you think he is the most "proud" of? He enjoys them both, but he takes no pride in the one that was given, only in the one that was earned. I learned the hard way that I shouldn't just give a car to my oldest son. He didn't appreciate it, he ended up abusing it, and most of the time just let it sit in the driveway because he refused to pay the insurance required so that he could drive it. Now he's grown up and on his own and harkens to the days when extravagant gifts were given to him. He now has to earn and pay his own way, but he appreciates everything he has now, even though it's far less than what he had when he lived at home with me. The car I gave him just didn't mean anything to him because he had no "skin" in the game. It is nice to get a gift, but that feeling of getting something you don't deserve is nothing compared to the feeling of getting something you've worked your ass off for. Eventually we all have to learn this lesson, and it definitely applies to talent.

Now I can't speak for you, but personally I would rather my creative abilities be a product of my hard work and personal development than to have come in the form of a "gift." In short, no one "gave" me the ability to write. I started off writing very poorly, and developed the skill over a lifetime.   Does that mean you have to spend a lifetime of development before you can create something worthwhile? Absolutely not! If you apply yourself, you can create great art today, tomorrow and next week, but more importantly, you will get better and better over the years until you have achieved mastery.

All I'm trying to say is that skills are hard earned whereas talent is generally "handed out" by the unjust hand of chance. If you truly believe that your ability to create is solely reliant upon the whim of chance as it has doled out your measure of talent, then stop reading and send this book back in to the bookstore or wherever, and get your money back. But, if you instead *choose* to believe that your ability to create is dependent upon your skills which you have acquired, studied to achieve, mastered and employed to great and lasting effect, read on my friend and thereby find peace and solace in these words.

We all love the myth of the overnight success, or of the child prodigy who just naturally succeeds because of a "gift." But most often it is just that… a myth. Tiger Woods is often regarded as a child prodigy. I would disagree and say his greatest gift was having been blessed with a father who trained him to develop a super-human work ethic. He practiced a minimum of eight hours a day for over ten years before he ever won his first event. Do you think maybe he had moments of doubt around year eight? How about year nine? Do you think Tiger Woods ever thought this pro-golfing thing may be a pipe dream? Somehow I doubt it, but moreover, I doubt it would have mattered. And the reason I doubt that it would have mattered is because when you love something enough to do it everyday all day for years and years with no guarantee that it will ever pay off financially, *that* is loving it enough to do it for the rest of your life for free. I practiced guitar everyday for as many as twelve hours a day for at *least* ten years, and if I had it to do over again, I would've practiced longer and harder. Not because I've made a good living at it, but because I loved every minute of it and now that I'm a grown up, I miss that level of mastery that only comes when you have the time to play your instrument as if it were your job.

What about the scores of artists and songwriters who burst onto the scene with enormous success seemingly overnight? By and large, the phenomena of the overnight success occurs only after about ten thousand hours of preparation. I have the privilege of working with several artists in Nashville who have been and will probably continue to be very successful in the music business. Two in particular are very likely to be household names within the next several years. How do I know this? Because both have been working their asses off tirelessly for the last ten years. Success is a marathon not a sprint. But what about the Justin Beibers of the world? Their success seems effortless? What about the people who are just born with it? Who have the right name? The right pedigree? Isn't that a factor? No, not really… Even a guy like Justin Bieber who burst onto the scene at age thirteen, was working feverishly and with unbelievable focus since the moment he could carry a tune, probably age four or so. So let's just say he worked hard for eight years before he had a hit record. He wasn't born with it. He worked for it. Maybe in 200 years Justin Bieber will have been the Mozart of our generation. It could happen...

So what about Mozart? Every time I try to dispel the myth of the child prodigy I get Mozart thrown up in my face, and usually the person in question is basing their entire body of knowledge on the movie *Amadeus*. Because obviously Hollywood could never, ever exaggerate historical fact in order to make a character more interesting.... Hmmm, If Mozart were alive today, he would be like Michael Jackson or Prince, no doubt, but people have built an unrealistic and super-human set of characteristics around the man that are actually quite unlikely. No one can deny that he was a creative genius, but did you know that Mozart practiced piano so much that his hands were physically deformed? As a therapist I have seen this phenomenon in fighters, martial artists as well as musicians. It is called carpal bossing. The human body responds to repeated stress by creating what is essentially "scar tissue" on the bones. The build-up can be quite significant. I once met with former World Heavyweight Champion Leon Spinx. His hands were enormous to begin with, but the joints of his knuckles had dense layers of calcium deposited from years and years of punching. From what descriptions I have heard of Mozart, this is what his hands looked like. They were essentially deformed from thousands of hours of relentlessly pounding on the piano, creating the muscle memory that made his work look effortless.

And what about his work ethic? Did you know that it was off the charts? Mozart wrote to a close friend once, frustrated that no one truly understood or appreciated the amount of **work** he put into his music. Mozart actually expressed frustration at the fact that people didn't really understand his genuine and relentless **effort**. As entertainers, all people really want to see is how easy we make it look. When they see us make it look easy, they assume it *is* easy. They don't see or understand the grit, determination, work, and pure and unadulterated abuse that we put ourselves through to reach a level of mastery where we can make it look so easy.

Even in his day Mozart was portrayed as having music pour forth from his mind as if he were taking dictation from God himself. Personally, I believe that if Mozart were alive today, he would be disappointed and even offended by the common belief that he was some sort of super-human. Imagine a garden in your back yard perfectly trimmed, manicured, neat, tidy, orderly and pristine. Imagine spending your lifetime growing and caring for it, obsessing over every last detail. How would you feel if everyone assumed that it just grew that way on its own? That is the curse of the genius. Other's cannot imagine doing the work that it takes to achieve that level of mastery, so they assume the genius has something that they do not and cannot possess. Mozart obviously felt it.

He was definitely the best of his time because he was very well educated in music, grew up with a brilliant and hard-working father who trained him and fostered his natural curiosity and developed his talents with relentless focus and practice. He was the very best because he worked the hardest, and that's the truth. Everything else you've heard about him, take it with a grain of salt... We love to exaggerate our heroes then worship them, and in my opinion that's what has happened to the legend of Mozart. If you are still dubious of my demands upon reason in this matter, then consider this... Everyone has heard Mozart's 25th symphony. It is a masterpiece by far and away, but has anyone ever heard his first? What about number two? Third time was a charm? No.... For Mozart the 25th time was the charm for symphonies. Yes, we all know his greatest hits, but for every hit there are a dozen *deep album cuts*. Some of it is actually tedious and boring to listen to. Now don't get me wrong, I'm not trying to taint the fact that Mozart was and is awesome, I'm simply trying to do him the honor of being realistic about the work that he put in so that he could write hits like the tune to "Twinkle Twinkle Little Star." Two hundred years later, we still sing our ABC's to a tune he wrote.

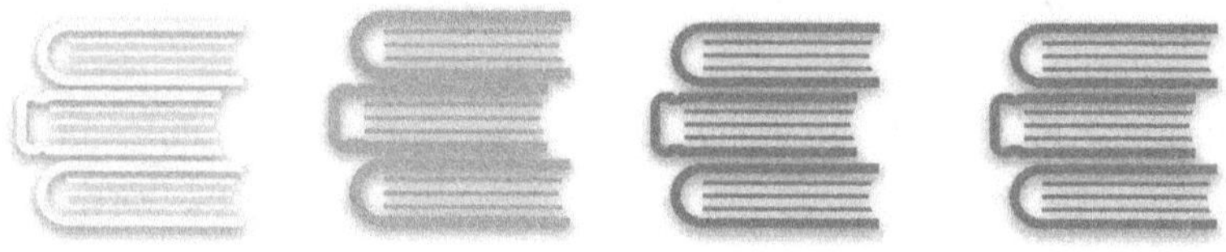

Yes he was a genius, but he was a genius who wrote over 600 pieces that we know about and he died at age 35, having begun his professional career at age five. That means that for 30 years, he composed about 20 pieces per year without a MacBook Pro. That's just slightly over one piece per month and some of these compositions were operas and symphonies of amazing instrumentation and complexity while some were short and sweet. If he had been writing pop songs, that number might have been much higher, like 20 pieces per month, but if you just look at the whole body of work and the time it took to complete it, it's actually quite doable. It was clearly genius, but not super-human. The average writer today writing full-time with all of the tools we have at our disposal might be able to quadruple the lifetime known musical output of Mozart.

My guess is that for the first twenty years or so, the majority of his work never saw the light of day. Have you ever written a song that was just too bad to share with others? If we continue with the assumption that Mozart was a human being, we have to assume he did the same at least on some level early in his development. Yes he wrote when he was just a child, but his father was there too, and most likely he was helping him in the early years. Even a genius would've had to learn to write, play, talk, perform, etcetera. Bottom line here is this… Mozart was probably no more of a superhuman than you are. He probably had no more talent than you do. What he had was an amazing work ethic which was the result of a lifetime of extremely disciplined effort with very little monetary reward. Sound familiar? He didn't do it for the money, he did it for the art, he loved the work. He probably felt he had no choice but to do the work. For a lover of music, what were his alternatives?

You can continue to believe that your heroes possess some magical gift that you do not, giving yourself the "out" that you need to be okay with failure, or you can begin today to *know* and understand the following; that it is the *work and consistency* that matters the most, and really and truly begin your journey in earnest. It's as simple as this… I am giving you the tried and tested methods for achieving success and even stardom which have been employed successfully by the vast majority of artists in the entertainment industry, including Mozart as far as we know. If you want to see your creativity soar, you have to develop your skills. Touch your heart and make this commitment to your craft.

I will work to develop the
skills necessary to succeed

You can look at the thousands of success stories and pick out the mere handful who got there through what you see as luck and ease or a family connection and come to the conclusion that you cannot do it, or… you can knuckle down, realize and understand the truth… that life is indeed far more fair than you might have been previously willing to admit. And today, begin the long hard road to success that is made up of a four letter word… no, not the one you're thinking of, this one. W… O…R…K. Every moment you waste cursing your luck in life or your lack of the right name or natural talent could be instead spent on working for the skills that will almost always eclipse those of the talented and lazy. Which brings me to my next topic.

No one can arrive from being talented alone, work transforms talent into genius.

<u>-Anna Pavlova</u>

Secret # 6

Do Not Rest On Your Talent

When I was a kid, I wanted to be a songwriter but someone close to me told me that I needed to have talent for that, and I just didn't have it. As a kid I was often told to give up on certain dreams and aspirations. I was told that the competition was too stiff, I wasn't smart enough, talented enough, or some other factor was out of my control and would always keep me at the level in which I found myself in life. I feel so lucky that I was too hard headed to listen to those naysayers. I think back at all the negativity I grew up with, all the despair and discouragement that was heaped upon me and I'm thankful that I was not smart enough to listen to those people. I'm glad I didn't have sense enough to settle for the status quo like I was told. Sometimes being dumb as a box of rocks pays off.

My talent is nothing without the skills I have worked hard for

I was recently at an event where a young lady approached me and wanted to know about my career and achievements. We spoke at length about life and dreams. She made this statement to me with an offhand gesture, "I know my dreams have to be realistic." I stopped her immediately and said, "Where in the world did you hear that nonsense?" Her statement struck me dumb for a moment. Dreams by definition should be fantastic. Dreams should be vast, grandiose. You should reach for the heights in your dreams. Dreams are no place for realism. If you're going to be realistic, why bother dreaming at all? Dream big, make your dreams your goals because after all, a goal is nothing more than a dream with a deadline.

Do not endeavor to be realistic with your dreams

You can actually be too talented for your own good… I for one, do not have that problem. I'm sufficiently obstinate that I have to learn hard lessons over and over before I get them. I have to fight tooth and nail for the victories I've achieved. I have to write multiple drafts of everything. I'm glad I have to work so hard for my product because I have come to realize that without all that work, the product has little meaning.

Writing is a tedious process for me, but it is also one of the most rewarding of all. Have you ever heard of some super talented celebrity who comes along, takes the world by storm, then walks away to do something else? It is possible to be too talented. In my music school over the past 20 years, I have seen many, many students come and go. The most talented people I have ever taught are no longer in the business of writing, performing or even playing an instrument. As a teacher, it used to be heartbreaking for me to see it. I'm sure many teachers reading this book can relate. We look back wistfully upon the memory of the amazing things we taught these children just to have them choose to turn to the dark side and get a real job when they could've been truly great as a writer, singer, composer, or entertainer.

I've come to the point in my life where I want to help people overcome their fears and inadequacies and become everything that they can possibly be as creative people who can go out and make a difference in the world, but I don't take it personally when they fail to meet my expectations. My expectations are as grandiose as my dreams, but my expectations of others must be tempered in reality.   I can't take it personally when a student considers the price tag of success to be just too high. Ultimately, every creative person has to make the choice to create. Every writer is on a journey. I don't control your journey… you do. You are the author of your own story. But I sure hope you make it a great one! Touch your heart and say it out loud…

Any student who is what I would call, "super talented." Often grows very bored with their talent very quickly. Why? Because they didn't have to work very hard to achieve what they have created and therefore do not experience that feeling of "reward" which most of us get through achievement. Remember my kid's gaming system? It's the same principle, I've often seen kids walk away over and over again from extraordinary talent because it failed somehow to deliver that feeling of reward.

One of the most profound tragedies of my children's generation is the "everybody gets a ribbon/trophy" philosophy. Never has a widespread social experiment gone so horribly wrong in my opinion. I mention this at the risk of sounding like one of those, "back in my day" people. I'll just say this… back in my day, life was not so good, and many things were brutal and harsh and well, just harder when I was a kid. I do not long for the days of no air conditioning, no internet, and when child abuse was the rule rather than the exception, but removing competition from a child takes a major life-long motivating factor and tosses it out the window. Most children need competition… they crave it, they feed off of it. Anyone who has ever observed more than one child at play can attest to this fact. You cannot stop children from competing, and everyone can't win all the time. We are not all the same, but healthy competition highlights our strengths and can be the compass which sets us all onto paths of personal success and achievement. I will say it again…

Competition can contribute to healthy development

We currently live in a society that seems to believe we should avoid competition. Sure, I understand that people want to shelter their children from those feelings of loss, I would not call defeat a pleasant feeling, but just because something is unpleasant does not mean that it is not benefitting you. The whole idea that for something to be beneficial it must be pleasant or pleasurable is complete horse-shit. If that were the case, why go to the gym? Why go to school? Why strive to be stronger, faster, better, more productive, more attractive? If people didn't have to strive to outdo one another, we wouldn't have air conditioning or internet or the automobile, women wouldn't wear makeup and men wouldn't shower nearly so often. By denying your children or yourself access to this critical motivator, you are in essence, dooming yourself and/or them to a lifetime of mediocrity.

So seek out competition and rivalry among your peers, it promotes growth and accountability. Saying you're going to write a song a day is one thing, but telling it to another songwriter and challenging her to do the same is something else entirely.   I recommend you do this, make it interesting, place a wager then get together in a week and compare songs.   Have another friend judge your lyric sheets anonymously and give you each feedback with a "grade" at the top of the page. This can get brutal if you have thin skin, but it's totally worth it. Besides, if you have thin skin, you need to get over it and fast. Let's be realistic, if you are more concerned about your feelings than the quality of your product, you need to find another business. Welcome critique and learn what you can from it. If you think a critique is unfair, biased, or unintelligent, find someone else and try again, but the chances are, if you don't like a critique… there's something to learn there, and you need to suck it up and learn it. I'll say it again.

Seek out competition and critique and learn from it

One of the most skillful songwriters I ever met was very early in my career. This guy had written a few songs with a local band, one of which had a very respectable regional hit and sold quite a few records, debuting on the rock charts in the top 10 and garnering major label attention which landed the band a record deal. This kid sat down with me and played song after amazing song, literally dozens, and all of them sounded like hits. I was astonished. I asked the kid it he would like to write together he just said, "nah, I'm bored with it. I just want to start my own company now." He had written all of these songs as "a hoot." He had done it when he was in his teens, and just didn't see it as challenge enough to hold his attention. At the time, I would've killed to have his talent, but in retrospect, I wouldn't want his talent at all. Not if, along with it came complete boredom with the craft. We all think we would like to have the talent that would make our craft easy, but if truth be told, that talent would doom us never to actually use it. Steve is an example of a super-talented, super-lazy guy. If he ever got his work ethic up to the level of his wit, he would be an unstoppable force, but he is quite content napping his way through life, penning a half-dozen songs a year and cursing the awful fortune life has dealt to him. Oh did I mention, Steve is unhappy and is quite bitter as well? Keep reading and I will explain why this iconic ultra-successful songwriter is so miserable, and perhaps you can avoid the pitfalls. Basically, Steve does not find his job rewarding… don't be a Steve.

Ask any person who has been doing their job for many years, be it educator, professional, creative, or entrepreneur, why they do what they do and they will say because it is "rewarding." If a job is not rewarding, you will not be happy doing it and if you have other options, more often than not, you will take them. A person who does not have to work simply cannot stay the course. So, if you feel you went through the *hard-headed* line twice and skipped the *talent* line, good for you. There's hope that you will be a great and mighty writer of songs and/or prose in the future. The creative genius works as if he has no talent... for you are one of the lucky few. So touch your heart and say it out loud...

I must work as if I have no talent

Adversity reveals genius, prosperity conceals it.

-*Horace*

Secret #7

Promote Connectivity

Let's take a look at how the brain works to create. In so understanding this complex mechanism, you can harness and channel your creative potential. You can easily identify what you're doing right and what you are doing wrong, tweak your habits and see your productivity increase exponentially. You may be thinking… why am I reading a science text book? If this is you, bear with me and you may be pleasantly surprised.

Amazing advances have recently been made in neuroscience which have expanded our understanding of how we create. It is imperative to understand what's new and dispel the age old myths that may be holding you back.   Greater understanding leads to greater power.

Knowledge is power

How many times have you been told… "the right brain is the creative center?" There must be a zillion books out there that insist that the right side of the brain is responsible for all creativity. Google it, and you will find a host of authoritative responses, all of which… I believe, are mistaken - or at least, incomplete.

I've always thought this was a load of malarky, but in school I kept my head down and answered appropriately on the test as I thought to myself, *if this is true, then why are the most creative people in the world left-brain dominant?* I've always held my suspicions that there was much more to the subject than this simple explanation of hemispherical dominance.

One of my songwriting mentors in Nashville, a man with millions of album sales to his credit recently had a stroke which severely impaired his brain function and coordination and yet he is still able to write songs at a very high level even though he now lacks the coordination to play the guitar at all. The right side of his brain suffered a devastating insult, but it has not had a significant impact on his creativity. He continues to work as a successful songwriter and educator.

As a therapist, I've worked with multiple people who have suffered all kinds of brain injuries and impairments including strokes, Alzheimer's, and traumatic brain injury and I have seen no clear and consistent or even anecdotal evidence of the above assertion that creativity is significantly influenced by hemispheric dominance. There are certain parts of the brain which control specific functions, and the right motor cortex controls the left side of the body and vice versa, but as far as creativity, it is not clearly associated with one side or the other. In my experience, a brain insult of any kind while it is specific in its effect on sensation and motor function, it is sort of *random* in its effect upon creativity. To me, this suggests that creativity is associated with "global" brain function versus hemispheric specificity. Furthermore, there are many imaging studies that support this assertion and suggest that connectivity exercises during stroke rehabilitation can help restore function following severe brain insults such as stroke and traumatic brain injury. As a therapist, we use this principle everyday in practice with stroke patients… and it works.

Most recent studies would suggest that there is a *connectivity* factor that plays the crucial role in brain function overall, and more specific to our discussion… upon creativity. Leading neuroscientists continue to study this concept called *neuroplasticity* as it plays a major role in all sorts of brain injury and disorders. I'm not writing a scientific journal here, so I won't bore you with all the details, I'll just say this. Significant evidence exists to support these assertions which you can easily find with a quick search at PubMed if you've a notion to do so. That being said, we will focus on greater connectivity as a means to boost your creative output.

It is not the development of one side or the other of your brain which stimulates creativity, it is rather, the way your entire brain communicates with itself, makes new connections and makes more effective connections possible which augments and accelerates creativity. That being said, what does it mean to you, the creative genius? Glad you asked…. In order to augment and accelerate your personal creativity we must promote connectivity in your brain.

I have often described songwriting as putting together a jigsaw puzzle where you get to make up the pieces yourself.   It's not just a 2 dimensional puzzle on a tabletop, no that would be far too simple. A song involves many elements including dynamics, attitude, pitch, groove, melody, harmony, thoughts, ideas, and the perceptions of both the performer and the audience, and probably a lot more that aren't obvious to me at the moment. These elements are analyzed during the writing process and performance and production strategies are brought into play to manipulate the overall message of the song. These are all connections your brain must make sense of as you write, and all of these elements are not formed in a single region of the brain.

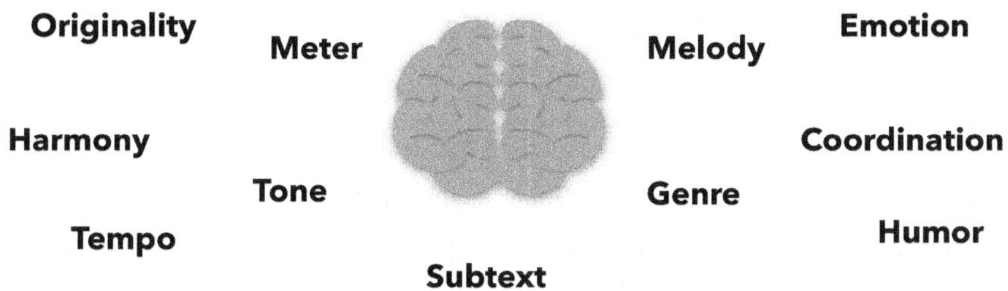

Sometimes as songwriters, we do a great job of this, but often we are lacking in one way or another. Adjusting even slightly, any one of these many elements can drastically alter the meaning, feel, or emotional connection that we have with a song. This is why writers, artists and producers of every sort have a lot of difficulty relinquishing creative control. Any deviation from the version of the product we hear in our heads or see in our minds can be very disturbing. If you don't understand and expect these feelings, it can lead to problems working with co-writers, producers and other artists. I've seen an artist walk out of the studio over a disagreement over a tempo. Once in a recording session with Steve, he called a halt over the whole studio to correct one single word of his song which the artist was apparently singing wrong. He kind of made an ass of himself over it even though *he* would not have thought so, and as a result, the artist never recorded another one of his songs. I thought it was a power play. She went on to have some success, so that little episode could well have cost him future album cuts. So choose your battles wisely... Don't be a Steve.

Simply the *way* a song is delivered can often bring a whole new meaning to the audience which the writer may not have originally intended. Putting together a song is the thoughtful combination of dozens of elements to form a meaningful work of art. It is an incredibly complex task, but a worthy one and when done well, it feels positively exquisite. So here I have explained the importance and the role of connectivity in creating the song, so now lets explore some strategies you can use to increase your connectivity.

During our daily routines, we tend to primarily use our dominant side for most tasks. As we have previously established, while the creative process does not occur in only one side of the brain, most of us are right hand dominant, right foot dominant and right eye dominant. This means that most of the tasks we perform throughout our days primarily stimulate the dominant sides of our brains. So, if you are right handed, your left brain is getting all the action and stimulation while your right brain is stuck mimicking what the left brain is doing, so poor right brain is always a step behind (if you are right handed).

Practice ambidexterity

The obvious solution... as creative people, we must force ourselves to use our non-dominant hand. The more connections you create, the more you stimulate every part of your brain and shake off the cobwebs. For instance, I hold my toothbrush and fork with my left hand, I place my glass on my left and use my left hand to drink. If you are really brave, try mousing for a day with only your non-dominant hand. If you put this book down now and do only this one thing, it will change your life. Even if you read no further, make it your mission in life to do this one thing every day. There are many hemispherical dominance tests available online. I recently took a few and found that my brain is virtually split down the middle. I essentially don't have a dominant side to my brain. I suspect that many other creative people are the same way after years of the following practice:

Force yourself to use your non-dominant side daily

Have you ever been in driving when severe weather struck suddenly? If you're like me, you get nervous and other cars on the road slow down and even stop because of near panic. Usually, you immediately turn off the radio, put both hands on the wheel and adopt an erect posture in your seat, placing yourself on high alert. The reason for this is that driving is a rote task, or something that has been repeated so often that we do it automatically. It is so routine and habitual that we really don't have to pay all that much attention in order to do it safely. Have you ever found yourself pulling up in your driveway after a long commute and suddenly realize you don't recall the last thirty minutes of driving? Scary feeling huh? Don't be alarmed, you were probably safe because your brain was on autopilot due to the years of repetition. But what is it about the rain or snow or hail beating down, the decreased visibility and slowing vehicles all around that causes us to nearly panic? The introduction of the additional stimuli have taken this familiar task which is normally rote, and has made it a very unfamiliar and therefore a cognitively taxing task.   All of a sudden, driving is no longer something you can do automatically, it is a task which requires all of your concentration and your life and those of your passengers depend upon it. That fear you feel at that moment is the defense mechanism that all humans depend on for survival.

Tasks that are very familiar are usually performed with the dominant hand, and for most of us, that is the right hand. When you switch a task that you normally perform with your dominant hand over to your non dominant hand, what happens in your brain at that moment is similar to what happens when the rain starts pouring down while you're trying to drive home. You take that rote task of brushing your teeth, and you make it a task that you have to think about. Try pouring the milk with your non-dominant hand, but have a towel ready. I wouldn't go out and start throwing darts at the pub just yet. Start with something less dangerous and work your way up. Every time you do, you are stimulating your non-dominant hemisphere, and that is a wonderful thing.

Ever forget where you put your keys when you get home? You are on autopilot, you walk in and they just go somewhere in the world and you don't think about it much till the next day when you need to get out the door. Try this... deliberately place your keys in your non-dominant hand when you walk in your house and set them down. Because you have taken this rote task and turned it into a deliberate task, you will remember exactly where you put them. You won't be able to forget. You can use this technique to hone your memory. The next time you really need to remember something, write it down with your non-dominant hand and see how it works for you.

Another proven method of promoting new connections in the brain is forcing yourself to do uncomfortable activities or tasks. The reason we gravitate to certain tasks is because they are familiar and comforting to us. We all love to do things that are fun and familiar, but what about activities we don't really want to engage in? I try to force myself to try new things whenever possible. I recently went out and tried a very unfamiliar sport… golf. I tried it a few times many years ago and was told to give it up as I just had no talent for it. Of course at the time I was young and stupid enough to believe it. But the truth was, I just didn't have much interest in it or any other sport. It just never was my thing, sports I mean. For that reason it was a very uncomfortable thing for me to try so when the opportunity to play was offered to me, of course I jumped at it. I have to admit that it was soothing in a way to have to listen to someone else's instructions, do exactly what they told me and concentrate. The whole time I was golfing I kept telling myself, *just relax and do as you're instructed*. I'm not saying that I will be a regular golfer now, but I can say that I actively engaged in an activity which was very uncomfortable for me. Obviously we all don't have time to take up multiple new activities that would suck more productive capital from our days. We obviously have to make deliberate decisions as to when and how we spend our time, but it is almost always a good idea to try a new thing whenever you can. It will awaken a new section of your brain in a way that a familiar task cannot.

Engage with the unfamiliar and uncomfortable

There are many brain games out there as well. I truly do not like numbers. That is why I will print out and spend 10 or 15 minutes on a number puzzle at least once a week. I do not do these because I like them, I do them specifically because I do not like them. Every minute I spend engaged in this is like torture to me, but it stimulates a part of my mind in a way that nothing else can. When you feel you are in a rut, try forcing yourself to do something you hate for a few minutes… in the interest of the greater good. It's like going to the gym. We will discuss this concept in greater detail later in the book, so stay tuned.

Meaningful Connections

The concepts discussed in this chapter, when placed into practice, will expand your ability to integrate and access multiple portions of your brain simultaneously. Practice these methods in order to achieve greater efficiency and expand and enhance your creativity. You will find that, as your ability to make new and more abundant connections in your brain develops and grows more efficient, your output will increase because the connections will come with less effort. You won't have to think nearly as hard in order to complete more complex tasks. When you go to the gym and work out your arms, lifting a box at work is a piece of cake. Precisely the same process occurs when you exercise your mind.

There is no great genius without some touch of madness.

<u>-Aristotle</u>

Secret #8

Eliminate Negativity

Metacognition is a three dollar word for the concept of thinking about thinking. Some experts refer to this concept as mindfulness and while it is an element of meditation, it is so much more to the creative genius. There are many reasons why you should be mindful of what you say and think, not just when you meditate, but all the time. The problem with people is, most of them are negative when left to their own devices and will default to negativity. Why is this the case? I'm so glad you asked.

Fear is hard-wired into who we are as humans. Historically, the more we fear, the greater the chance for survival. Throughout human history with the exception of the last 100 years or so, human survival, not comfort... but *survival* was critically dependent upon our abilities to fear certain elements of our environment. If you were not afraid of hunger, you would starve. If you were not afraid of the winter, you would freeze. If you were not afraid of the predators, you would get eaten, and if you were not afraid of mortality, you would've never had children. Fear quite simply was a critical element for survival up until the modern age.

Now we, as civilized humans live fairly safe lives. We don't have to worry about starvation or predators by and large, but we are still held back by those hard-wired fears.   Because of those very primitive survival instincts, we are constantly talking to ourselves, filling our own heads with nonsense.   For the most part, we are using all of that creativity for the purpose of coming up with worst-case scenarios that will never-ever happen. How many times a day do you hear the phrase, "I'm afraid that…" Probably more than a few I'll bet. Now we aren't complete idiots, I mean people aren't afraid of a saber-toothed tiger. Although fearing such a beast would be just as productive as fearing that someone at work is going to hurt your feelings. Or fearing that someone is going to say something negative about your hairstyle or about the jeans you are wearing. Fear in short is… for the most part, useless to the creative genius. It is colossal waste of time and brain power.

Fear is a waste of time

The problem with all those fears is they crowd your mind and take up much needed creative energy. People come up with the most creative if not ridiculous fear-based scenarios about what awful thing is about to happen, all day every day. The cumulative brain power that is wasted on negative thinking is nothing short of staggering.

Consider this example… Imagine there is a hydro-electric plant which produces the electricity which powers your home. Your electric bill is 100 bucks a month, not bad, the only problem is.. You find out that the manager of the plant is just releasing 80% of it's power into the air where it serves absolutely no purpose. Wouldn't you be outraged? If your plant manager wasn't wasting that electricity, your bill could probably be 20 bucks a month. Currently that is what is going on in your mind and it really should piss you off!

Just imagine if you could literally shut down that negativity and re-appropriate that intellectual power and creativity to produce ideas that will be useful to you in your craft. That is exactly what I am going to help you do. Get excited about it. You are about to become a creative dynamo with 100% of your intellectual power being directed to where you want it to go. You just have to reprogram your incredibly wasteful brain.

Whether you are religious or not, we can all relate to the concept of *faith*. Faith is basically believing that something good is going to happen. Fear is the opposite of faith. Fear is believing that something bad is going to happen. I can relate to someone having faith or hoping that something good will happen, but what purpose does fear serve? It may have been a good idea to have a lot of fear a thousand years ago, or even a hundred years ago, but now it's just clogging up your pipes. Why would you want to believe something bad will happen, it just doesn't make sense. It's counter productive and self sabotaging behavior. The creative genius should never indulge in this behavior. In the modern era, humans have gone from benefitting from fear, to being stymied by it. It is extremely important for the creative genius to conquer his fears if he is to flourish in the modern era.

To that purpose, you must be very careful of what you say to yourself. Most people are poor listeners, but the one person to whom you will listen and subsequently, believe practically anything they say is… you. You are your own worst enemy. Every bad thing that could possibly happen to you, you have most likely already dreamed up and lived in your mind. You must learn to let go of that negativity which you cherish so dearly. Those negative thoughts currently occupy cathedrals in your mind. We want to clear out those rooms and set up shop, allowing that useless and counterproductive energy to be instead, channeled into creativity. You guide your thoughts, they do not guide you. Touch your heart and say it out loud.

I rule my thoughts they do not rule me

The best way to battle against negative and unproductive thinking is to counter with a positive thought or action in the same way a boxer answers a punch with a counter-punch. For instance… Imagine you are getting ready to go into a songwriting session with someone whom you've never met.

Mr. Negative says: *You're not smart enough, your ideas won't be good enough, they're probably not going to like you anyway, you should just cancel.*

The creative genius says: *I am smart, I am capable, and I am well regarded. There is no reason why this should not be a productive meeting.* The creative genius just put the smack down on Mr. Negative. BOOYA!

And this is what you have to do all day every day until Mr. Negative finally withers and dies. Eventually you will not hear his voice, but it takes vigilance and relentlessly conscious effort to eradicate him. And when that happens, you free all that brain power that once negative energy had sapped from your intellectual capital. You free that vast space that would otherwise be wasted and re-appropriate it to instead, do your bidding. You can consciously redirect your energy toward a worthy and noble pursuit. You can do it. Touch your heart and say it with me…

I will conquer Mr. Negative

Sometimes the most important thing you can do in the area of your thinking is… not to think at all. This is harder than it sounds. We should, on a daily basis, shut down our thoughts entirely and do a "reboot." This is basically a meditation technique widely used by practitioners to achieve *alpha* waves in the brain. I call these little sessions, mini-meditations. I do it for 10 to 15 minutes the first thing in the morning, then again several times throughout the day. You see, most people go through their day bouncing off the walls from distraction to distraction, watching television, staring at a computer, a cell phone, or engaging other people literally all day long with absolutely no lapse. We get home at the end of the day and we are mentally exhausted and oftentimes, incapable of having meaningful interaction or creative time. This can be extremely damaging to your personal relationships especially with your family.

Do this instead and it will work wonders for your creativity. Turn off all distractions, go someplace where you can be alone and limit or ignore all outside stimulation. I do this in my car sometimes. You can do it with your eyes open or closed, dealer's choice… I have actually ducked into a dark closet in the oddest places before and just stood still for five or ten minutes and just forced my mind to stop thinking. It refreshes your intellect like you cannot quite understand until you've tried it. Most people in my life don't even know that I do this, but I do it often. I do it daily. Sometimes I know my wife must think I'm a complete goofball, but I don't care, she knows what she married…. If you care what people around you think about these techniques, then perhaps the people are the problem, not the techniques… food for thought.

Tell your smartphone to give you an alarm in 5 minutes so you will know when to stop without being distracted by looking at a clock. Later you can increase to 10 or 15 minutes as you get better at it. Find an object far away in the distance and stare directly at it and think of nothing. Clear your mind. Focus on your intellect, listen to the sound of the air entering and exiting your lungs. Thoughts will come and go, just let them float by and ignore them. Look at the object in the distance but don't concentrate on it, just use it as a focal point for your undistracted and complete concentration. Focus on the feel of the rise and fall of your chest, feel the breath as if fills your lungs, let it exit effortlessly as you relax your diaphragm.

As soon as you hear the alarm, pick up your phone, or a pen and paper and start writing down everything that pops into your mind. Don't stop to overthink what you are writing. You subconscious has continued working while your conscious mind was relaxing. I look at it like this… I have shut down my conscious mind and "loaned" that creative power to my subconscious mind, allowing it to create without interruption. I think of my mind like a giant web which is catching all kinds of thoughts and ideas and making connections which I may have never made consciously.

Although we sleep, our brains don't shut off. Your subconscious mind continues to have a field day while you are conked out, and quite often, it is working out all the problems that you couldn't consciously solve throughout the day. It is important to "tune in" to these thoughts and harness the power of that part of your brain and capture the time you spend sleeping… Think of it, you spend one third of your life sleeping and by and large, you are unaware of what your brain is doing. What would you say if I told you that you can use your sleeping unconscious mind like an assistant?

For years, every night before I go to sleep, I give my brain a project to work on while I'm resting. And somehow, it listens and responds. Often times I will be stuck on a line of a song or a melodic idea that is bothering me, I lay down at night and silently tell my brain to work on it as I fall asleep, and very often, I will have that "eureka" moment the next morning. You may say "coincidence my good man, nothing but coincidence." Well all I can say to the naysayers is, first of all, what are you doing still reading this book? Secondly, coincidence is not magical thinking, it happens all the time and is quite common actually. Thirdly, if the same thing happens consistently, it is no longer a coincidence. My brain has continued to problem solve for me in the absence of consciousness. It happens several times a week. Call it what you want, it works. You too can train yourself to do the same. In a later chapter, I will take you through a day in the life of the creative genius and I will demonstrate to you the precise technique you can use. If it works for me, it will work for you too.

If you are delusional, sometimes the reality catches up with your delusion, and then all of a sudden you are a genius.

-Jason Calacanis

Secret # 9

Expect Creative Success

We all love those moments of spontaneous genius. That feeling when you know you are onto an amazing idea and all you have to do is hang on and ride it till the song writes itself. Those are great feelings, but it doesn't happen that way every time. Those moments come, but not nearly as often as we would like.   For most of us those "eureka" moments are few and far between. But what if you could *feel* that way every day, wouldn't that be awesome? Well you can! The beautiful thing about feelings is that we can create them, and oftentimes, when the feeling comes, the moments of creative genius often follows.   I know it sounds like hocus-pocus, but bear with me a moment.

I want to try an experiment with you…. I want you to think of something that you want more than anything. It could be a fancy car or home, it could be an educational goal or a hit record, it could be love or a friendship. Whatever that thing is that you want more than anything get a clear picture of it in your head. Imagine what it would be like to hold it and touch it. Imagine what it would be like to drive it, smell it, taste it.   Imagine the *feeling* you would feel if you *already* had it. Actually stop reading and do this now before proceeding. Now, do you feel that smile creeping across your face when you imagined you already had that thing that you want?   Did you feel that feeling of euphoria?

You may not have that thing… yet, but the *feeling* you just experienced is the *real* thing…. It isn't any less real because you created it. After all, you are the creative genius.   Now…. Let's do the same thing with a song, or a work of art or a story. Imagine that song is written already, imagine that it is in the can. Imagine your producer and your favorite artist shaking your hand and congratulating you on your unbelievable success with this song.   Imagine receiving your song of the year grammy and what you look like on TV in your tuxedo or evening gown as you thank your friends and professional support system. Feel the warmth and appreciation of your audience. Imagine your family calling and texting you to congratulate you. You may not have it yet, but that *feeling* is real. You can feel it every day, but why do it?

This is an exercise called positive realization.   The purpose is to generate the feelings of success and happiness that you want and need in your life.   By doing this exercise daily, you are getting your mind and body ready for the success that will come when your creativity blossoms. You are preparing your mind to receive the things you want more than anything.   You are telling the universe your deepest desires and wishes. You are being honest with yourself about what you really want out of life. In so doing, you are actually clarifying to the universe what it is you really and truly want.

I have found this exercise to be very helpful to me in overcoming negative thoughts, feelings and emotions. By consciously choosing to feel these positive feelings and emotions, you are actively blocking out the default negativity that would otherwise dominate your mind. In my life, I have actually practiced this exercise and have had miraculous results before, and there are many people out there who swear by the method.   Even if you are skeptical about prayer, or meditation, or telling the "universe" what you want, you can still use this practice as many other creative people have… to create positivity and visualize the success that you want and deserve. I am not asking you to "believe" in anything, all I ask is that you try it. Go through the motions and see how it makes you feel. See if your positive realizations produce results. You may be surprised but even if you do not have some miraculous results, you can still benefit from all the positive feelings that you have produced in your mind.

For many humans, negative is default

Personally, I have found that when I begin a writing session by slipping into the men's room and going through this practice and creating these positive feelings, oftentimes the "eureka" moment actually follows quite closely.   It's a chicken versus the egg thing.   Sometimes when you create the egg, the chicken will appear. When my boys were little, I used this method with them, and while on one hand they couldn't stand it, on the other, they have each eventually come to appreciate the practice and use it to this day. Its quite simple and it goes like this… smile. Are you crying? Are you angry? Are you disappointed? It doesn't matter… force a smile onto your face and hold it there till it feels natural. Often when one of my boys would come to me with a problem and they were feeling negative emotions, I would order them to smile, then I would smile with them. After thirty seconds of this we would both be laughing at each other. At that point I would say, "now that we aren't feeling negative emotions we can work on solving this problem." To this day, it gets them every time.

Being an effective creator is more about balance than any other single factor. You can actually be disciplined about that balance in order to maximize results. Eureka moments occur when we are not thinking actively about the problem we wish to solve. Eureka moments spring from the subconscious. The subconscious mind never stops working, it is always running in the background and as creative people, we must put ourselves into the states of mind to allow our intellect and our creative minds to provide worthwhile output daily.

Eureka versus work ethic

Have you ever had that feeling where you were actively trying to force yourself to remember something that was right on the tip of your tongue? And the harder you tried to think of the thing that was bothering you, the further it seemed to get out of reach? The next time that happens, close your eyes and clear your mind. Force yourself to think about nothing for a few minutes and quite often, the solution will just "pop" into your head. This is something that happens spontaneously to us every now and then, but by "feeding" the subconscious mind and actively guiding ourselves into these alpha states several times a day, we can trick our conscious minds into "borrowing" that subconscious ability to make all those crazy connections that make high-level creativity possible.

Most creatives will experience periods of feast and famine. While some creatives claim to have had intense periods of creativity around tumultuous events in their lives. This occurs when the creators' mind is so preoccupied with what's going on in their lives that the subconscious is forced to work alone. As a result, *eureka* moments occur many and often. In contrast, a creative who is more focused on the craft of writing with a disciplined and more forceful approach will often neglect the subconscious mind's input, creating a deficit of ideas. This is the most common problem with creative people and the reason why so many songwriters are "stingy" with their ideas. By giving your mind the release it needs on a regular basis, you put your subconscious to work for you. When you do this consistently, the ideas will come so fast that you cannot write them all because your "crafty" brain cannot keep up. For the creative genius, this is the optimal situation. We want an abundance of song seeds at our disposal so that when your crafty brain is ready and willing to work, you can choose only the very best ideas to pursue.

Wouldn't it be nice to have periods of feast and greater feast? This is the optimum position to put yourself into. Isn't this what we all really want? Whatever it is that you really want, you can have it with the correct effort applied. There is no reason for you to idealize the success you want. Let me go a bit deeper here. Imagine someone who is the most successful person you can think of. For myself, it could be my favorite actor Al Pacino, my favorite entrepreneur Elon Musk, or it could be my favorite songwriter, Willie Nelson. It is important to understand deep down in your brain that all these people whom you idolize and put up on a pedestal are actually real people. Most any of the successful people whom you can name when you get right down to it are just like you and me. The key difference is their work ethic and the fact that they were fearless enough to attempt and continue attempting in a highly difficult and competitive field and succeed. Willie Nelson had enough failures to have stopped any other artist in their tracks a hundred times over. Have you ever heard his voice? Not exactly what I would call pretty, but oh my does it have charm.

When you regard successful people as *awesome*, it places what they do in an unattainable category. It makes what they do impossible to you in your mind and experience. And in case you haven't been listening, it all starts in your mind. If you cannot imagine the success you want, you will never be able to achieve it. So, dare to imagine the success you want, stop thinking of your heroes as some kind of super-humans. Think of them as people who have been doing what you want to do for a longer period of time. Think of them as people who have placed themselves in the paths of success more times than you have. Think of them as running the same race, but just having started before you. You must think of your heroes as having blazed the trail for you. Follow their successes and avoid their failures, but don't assume that you will never overtake them. Your success will never be greater than your ability to imagine it. So why not imagine the ultimate success for yourself?

Imagine The Success You Want

One of my favorite stories is one of a Navy fighter pilot who was shot down over North Vietnam during the war. Strictly speaking, whether the story is fact or legend I do not know, but the story illustrates a valuable principle. As the story goes, the POW was confined to a small cage for five years. Under these conditions almost anyone would lose hope. The only thing he could think of doing to occupy his mind was to play mental golf. He had been an avid golfer for many years and truly loved the game. So every morning he would close his eyes at exactly the same time and he would imagine that he was on a golf course back in the good old US of A. He would imagine getting dressed, grabbing his stuff, walking out to the course. He would imagine the perfect day, the wind direction, the cut of the grass, the temperature of the air. He would literally imagine every detail of the entire experience right down to each and every perfectly executed swing of his golf club and every absolutely perfect putt. He did this religiously each and every last day of his confinement. Eventually a prisoner exchange was arranged and he came home a much thinner man. He spent a few months in the hospital getting stronger, but eventually the day came when he returned to a real golf course where, in his very first round of golf he was astonished to find that he had shaved 20 strokes off his best game ever. Or so the story goes.

The point here is, whether you're a golfer, a painter or a musician, if you are incapable of dreaming-up your ultimate idea of success, you are incapable of making it a reality. Once I opened for Lynyrd Skynyrd in a large outdoor event. As I stepped off the stage to the roar of the largest crowd I had ever seen, let alone played in front of, a reporter came up to me and said, Doc I can't believe your performance. Is this the largest crowd you've ever been in front of? I told her yes it was by far. She said I can't believe how comfortable you were, it looked like you'd done it a million times. Pointing to my head I said, "Well, I have." Visualization is not hocus-pocus, it is a powerful tool. Use it. But don't take my word for it, just in case you're listening to yourself, touch your heart and say it out loud…

I will visualize the success I want daily

Tying It All Together

To the creative genius, creation equals success. You cannot separate the two concepts. In teaching the principles of the first, I also teach the principles of the latter and vice versa. If you find yourself asking the question, "is this book about creativity or success?" First ask yourself the following question: "For me, is it possible to achieve the one without the other?" To the creative genius, creativity is success and success is creativity.

True genius resides in the capacity for evaluation of uncertain, hazardous, and conflicting information.

— *Winston Churchill*

Secret #10
Focus!

Another important metacognition technique involves choosing *what* to think about and *when*. Most of us have a stream of consciousness which behaves like a flock of birds darting about and flitting from one direction to the other, the rest of the thoughts mindlessly following the leader like those birds. At least the birds are all basically following some leader. Others of us have a stream of consciousness which behaves more like a pit of snakes slithering about in every direction at all times, intertwining among themselves and twisting about aimlessly in the dark. Which are you? Hopefully from now on, neither!

The most desirable stream of consciousness for the creative genius involves self-directed metacognition. If you are to direct your flow of consciousness toward your goals and desires in life, you must be the absolute ruler of your thoughts. We've touched on this before, but now I want to add another layer of difficulty. Once you have mastered your negative thoughts, the next step is to master your positive thoughts. It's not enough just to eliminate the negative, to truly master your brain power, the creative genius must exercise authority over all thought processes. When this happens, you truly enter a state of productivity that most people aren't even aware exists.

Admittedly, unless you are some kind of monk with 50 years of meditation under your belt, I seriously doubt most of us will ever truly reach a level of *complete* mastery of our thoughts, but try your best and you will get better and better at it as you go along. As we discussed earlier, Mr. Negativity will wither and die, and the positive and more powerful you will continue to emerge. As you continue to master your thoughts, your goals will find a way and the universe will respond to you. Here's some ancient wisdom to ponder, and every religion has its own version of it, which to me gives credence to the truth of the principle, even if you disagree with individual ideologies. *As a man thinks in his heart, so is he.*

The technique I am about to describe will change your life if you apply it. It may seem, on the surface to be elementary or even simplistic, but once you have tried it you will discover just how difficult it is to master. Your mind is like a bull that will desperately try to buck off and dislodge any and all attempts to control it. For this reason, you should probably begin by trying to do this for 8 seconds at a time and work your way up from there, if you'll allow me to carry forward with the rodeo reference. Every time you get bucked off, get right back on. Here it is in essence… Keep your mind absolutely trained on whatever it is you are doing at the time you are doing it. Try it when you are brushing your teeth (with your non-dominant hand). Think only about brushing your teeth. Notice every detail, the feel of the brush in your mouth, the sting of the toothpaste, the vibration of the bristles against your teeth and gums. Your mind will desperately try to break away and wander off to some other random thought like a wayward toddler, but keep bringing it back to the moment you are in, no matter how many times it takes.

Be patient, be persistent. Master your mind to perform the simplest of tasks without interruption.

The next time you are in your car driving, bring your mind to bear on the task at hand. Feel the steering wheel in your hand. Feel the vibration of the road as it changes beneath you, listen to the hum of your tires on the pavement. Watch the cars around you intently. Check your mirrors. Turn off the radio and really bring your full attention to what you are doing. Stop the wheels of your mind from turning and force them to turn only to your will. Bring your mind under your own control and become your own master. This bears repeating, so touch your heart and say it with me…

I choose to become the master of my own thoughts

This is a great technique to use when you are doing something that would normally frustrate and annoy you. This is going to sound counterintuitive, but this is precisely what you should do if you have a job to accomplish and you really don't have time to do it. When you feel pressured and pressed for time, I know it sounds crazy, but slowing down in those moments of stress and really and truly focusing on the task in all of its fine and intricate details with 100% of your attention will make the task go much quicker. Stressing out over a deadline is the most sure fire way to miss it. Freaking out will lead to disaster. The job takes as long as the job takes, stressing about it will only make it seem to take longer and make you feel negative energy while doing it. Negativity kills your positive energy. We can't always control all the crappy jobs we have to do and we can't like them all, it's just a simple fact of life… but, we can control how we feel during these crappy tasks and we can use them to practice control of our own thoughts.

Personally, I do not enjoy housework and there was a time when I would do anything to distract myself from that work while I was doing it. I would turn on the tv or the radio, put in the earbuds and listen to a book or music… anything to distract me from it, but what I found out is this. My best efforts at distracting myself from my work only prolonged the work itself.   Once I focused on the task at hand and truly considered and concentrated on what I was actually doing, the time and the job verily flew by like the proverbial wind.

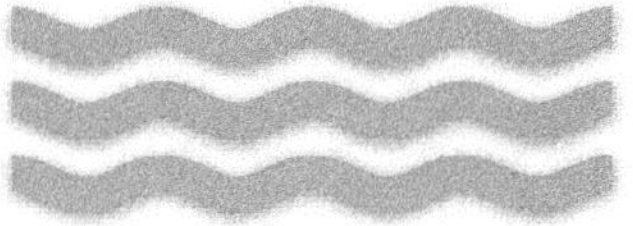

If you find yourself behind on a deadline, force yourself not to respond to the stress. Focus on the task and take your sweet time doing it. You will find that by removing the anxiety from the equation, your work flows like water down a stream. The water does not get in a hurry, it does not have a deadline, the water takes how long the water takes, no more, no less. You cannot hurry it, agitating it only interrupts the flow and delays the inevitable completion. Be like water.

Early in my career as a therapist I used to get really stressed out over my work. I would go into a building and have far more patients than I could possibly see in a shift. It would freak me out so much that my blood pressure would shoot up and I would have anxiety attacks. As a result, I would end up not only being upset all day and not enjoying my work, but I would also end up working hours of overtime and getting in hot water with my boss over that as well. To make matters worse, the added anxiety would cause me to make stupid mistakes that I just wouldn't normally make. My anxiety over my job back then made me think I had made a terrible life choice. I was miserable and my days would drag on for what seemed like an eternity, it was drudgery.

Be like water... flow

One day, as I was having one of my especially stressful moments a patient said, why don't you just stop worrying and start paying attention to what you're doing? After all, you'll never make a positive change with a negative attitude. Something inside me snapped with the realization that I was actually upsetting my patients with my bad attitude. My negativity was having a negative effect upon my ability to perform my job, and if truth be told it was affecting every other area of my life. At the time, I was working a full time job, a part-time job and still was carrying a student load of 30 private students at my studio plus a monthly recital and songwriting sessions on top of that. In addition, I was still performing in a regional act and traveling most weekends. In case you haven't figured this out, I love being busy. The problem was, I was letting the stress ruin my life. I decided right there that I was going to have to make a change and I figured that my patient's advice was as good a place as any to start. I made up my mind that my work was going to take how long it took and my getting upset about it would not change that simple fact.

The next day, I didn't even look at how many patient's I had, I just simply started with the first one and gave her my full, undivided attention and something magical happened... Time flew by. I saw the next patient and the next patient with my full and undivided attention on each and every one. I thought through every task and attacked each one systematically and methodically without ever consulting the clock. I remember the very first day of this I got to my last patient and had to go back and recount them.   I thought my caseload had shortened. I thought I must've missed someone. I had finished seeing each patient on my list stress-free and actually finished early. Gone was the anxiety and fear of not being able to get to everyone in time. Gone was the feeling of fear of my boss getting on to me for having to stay late. I discovered something of great importance that day. It was the stress itself that was holding me back, not any lack of time.   I was creating stress where none really needed to exist.

Whatever it is you are trying to accomplish, you can get more done faster and easier by putting your mind 100% to the task. The myth of multitasking is just that, a myth.   Anyone who claims they can do multiple things at once and get them all done with any degree of completeness and quality isn't just lying to you, they are lying to themselves. There are multiple randomized controlled trials which bear this assertion out, the science does not lie. If you choose to cling to the myth as if you are the exception, you do so at your own peril and to the collective peril of your creative abilities. Multitasking is unproductive for the vast majority of us, and underproductive for the rest. Only by truly focusing on each task individually and completely do you bring your intellect fully to bear on the work at hand. When you truly focus on what you are doing, you will rock and roll through your workload like you never thought possible.

Tying It All Together

I have found the principles discussed in this chapter to be especially true of music production. Often, as writers we find ourselves very anxious about deadlines. We often fear that we will never be able to produce on demand. This is, quite simply, a lie. As previously discussed, we listen to our minds too often when it defaults to negativity. If you are to harness and master your creative genius, you must learn this simple skill… Focus!

Genius is eternal patience

-Michelangelo

Secret # 11
Never, Ever Let an Idea Get Away

This book is not meant to cover the "craft of songwriting." So I will just cover enough to give the reader a sense of how creativity in songwriting goes hand in hand with the craftsmanship thereof. Perhaps the "craft" of songwriting will be covered in my next book. When I discuss the craft of songwriting, I am talking about the actually mechanical aspects of the song. Which are the parts of a song, elements of the song, how to assemble the song, etc. Like I said, this is a completely different discussion. However *craftsmanship* in general, applies to all creativity. The creative brain comes up with all the elements, while the crafty brain assembles them. There can be no work product without excellent craftsmanship. The creative genius understands the marriage of creativity and craft.

Think of the creative brain as building up a pile of bricks, lumber, nails, and shingles while the crafty brain builds the house. In songwriting, the two occur sometimes simultaneously, but not in my studio. Here is how I create a song most of the time… First, my creative brain comes up with what I call a "song seed." A song seed is just a basic concept for a song. It can be just a single word, a single line, a few lines, or even just a melodic idea. I write hundreds of song "seeds" a month generally speaking, but I may sit down in a single day and write several dozen at a time. You should write them really fast, and write them the moment they come, no matter what else is going on. I don't recommend even stopping to appreciate them because if you do, you may miss the next three great ideas that are right behind the one you are stopping to admire. Just let the ideas flow. These little ideas come from everywhere and you are surrounded by them all day everyday. All you have to do is listen for them. So make a commitment to yourself to catch every single idea that comes within your sphere of creativity. Touch your heart and say it out loud…

I will never let an idea get away

For instance, the other day I was talking to a guy while standing in line at a store. I said, "how's your day going?" And he replied, "you know… lather, rinse, repeat." I immediately took out my cell phone and jotted the idea down.   Does that mean I will write a song based on that concept? I'm not sure at this time, but it immediately struck me as a novel *concept* that *may* eventually "spin" into a hook in my brain at some point. Currently, my brain is mulling that idea over and over while I write, shower, eat, sleep, live, laugh and love. If I think it's worth writing down, I put my subconscious on it and let it percolate. In the next few chapters or so, I will reveal how this idea may develop into a better idea, then into the eventual song. If you think this idea, "lather, since, repeat." Is a dumb one, you are probably not alone, but personally I have a good feeling about it.   I don't know what my subconscious has in mind for this one, but I think it's going to be pretty cool.

Another thing that should be happening right now if you have been listening is… stop reading and deposit that idea into your "seed bank" if you are a songwriter. Why would I encourage you to "steal" my idea? Because it's just an idea. You can't copyright an idea, so why try. I can come up with a great idea, hand it to 10 different songwriters and get 10 entirely different songs that have nothing to do with each other. If you happen to touch on the same concept as I am going for with this idea, it would be a massive coincidence. So take it, write it. If you hear another idea and you think you can do a better job with it, take it, rewrite it, have fun with it, learn from it. Even when you write a bad song or an unoriginal song, you are still exercising the muscles which make you better at what you do. If you take the idea I just shared and write a better song than me, I wish you the joy of your accomplishment. If you are capable of writing a better song than me with it, then you deserve it! The only caveat I would add is to be careful not to "hook" the idea in the same way another writer has. Strictly speaking, it's not plagiarism, but it's kind of tacky. Something I used to do a lot when I was a young writer is to take other songs on the radio and try and write an "answer" to them. Another thing I would do is randomly pick a song out of a list and attempt to use the title to write my own song. It helps if you haven't actually heard the song you're borrowing the title from, but it's a good exercise for any songwriter. The majority of ideas you hear were the brain-children of a song that came before. Without the original song that some caveman hummed as he started his fire, we would have no music at all. All ideas are fair game, so use your peers and mentors as springboards, not mirrors. If I had a nickel for every original idea that I came up with, wrote a song thinking it was 100% absolutely grade A *my* brain-child and free from inspiration from any other source, only to turn on the radio and hear the exact same title slapped onto another song, I would... well I'd have a dozen or so nickels.

The point is, it happens. I'll give you an example. Back in 2009 my wife had roped me into watching this movie called "Sex In The City." It was absolutely awful and excruciating to watch, but at some point in the movie I heard a phrase spoken which was music to my ears. Upon awakening from her depression following a much-needed jilting at the hands of the roguish and handsome, "Big," Carrie coins the term, "Mexicoma" to describe her painful reverie. I immediately checked out of the movie and began writing the chorus of the song of the same title. I'll just share the chorus with you:

I'm in a Mexicoma

My baby's in Arizona

Stuck in Oklahoma

She left me here all alone-a

Cuervo Gold and Corona

My only friends in this

Whole damn time zone

Since she walked away

I've been passing the days

In A Mexicoma

Now, you may be thinking… *doesn't Tim McGraw perform a song of the same title?* You would be right. Many people who have heard both songs say mine is much better. So why did the other song get recorded by Tim McGraw and mine got recorded by me? I don't know and I don't care. I didn't bring it up to complain about it. It's just to let the reader know that it will happen. It may happen over and over again. It has happened to me many times in my career, but never before has it happened so overtly and famously. Obviously the writers who penned the Tim McGraw song were watching the same movie as me and got the same idea as I did. Now their song came out a good eight years after mine was written, but it very well could've been written at around the same time. It's also important to note that they took the same title and went a completely different direction with it. Every one of the songs you write serves a purpose, they are the bricks and mortar that build the experiences that make up who you are as a writer and an artist, and that makes every experience whether good or bad, quite worthwhile. Somebody asked me when that song came out if I was frustrated about it, I said "Absolutely not." On the contrary, I'm encouraged by the fact that I have the same artistic sensibilities and instincts as other writers who are getting Tim McGraw cuts. Bottom line is, I have hundreds of songs written, and most of them are even better than that one. If that song can get cut by Tim McGraw, I've got a hundred more that can. In any situation, we have a choice to become bitter or take the lesson and learn from it and move on. I choose the latter. That being said, there are many songs out there that have the same title. You can't copyright a title, and that means that all titles are fair game.

This same sort of thing happened to a good friend and co-writer of mine, Dave Stewart. Dave is famously called the "walking cowboy" because he actually walked from Gillette, Wyoming to Nashville, TN on what was essentially a dare from his wife on the *hope* that he would be allowed to fulfill his lifelong dream of playing on the Grand Ole Opry. He wrote a book about the experience which I highly recommend. It's quite a unique take on the concept of true grit and the power of intention. My friend actually walked over 1600 miles with no guarantee that he would even get to play the Opry. To find out how it turned out, read the book "Heart and Sole." Shortly after his arrival to Nashville, Dave found himself sitting in a waiting room talking to another gentleman who happened to be Toby Keith. Dave was telling his story about walking to Nashville and mentioned his book which he was thinking of calling "Dream Walking." A year later, Toby Keith released his new single… you guessed it, *Dream Walking*. As Dave and I discussed this situation, all I could think was… "Why the heck didn't he use that same title to write a song?" Of course it wouldn't have been the same song, it may or may not have even been as good as Toby Keith's song but that's not the point. The point is, it was a great idea for a song that Dave had in his possession and he never even recognized it as such. It's like finding out you had been walking around with the Powerball jackpot-winning ticket in your pocket having never even known it. How many tickets do you let get away from you? Food for thought.

I challenge you to do a browser search for popular song titles and as randomly as you can, pick ten out and write them down. Choose only songs that you have never heard and have no idea of the lyrics or the melody except of course for the title. If necessary, go to another genre to choose your titles. Once you have chosen them, for the next ten days, pick one title and write down ten different ways that each title can be "hooked." What are the various angles that you can attack that title from? Are there any clever plays on the words in the title? Can you tweak it a bit and make the title your own? Once you have performed this brainstorm exercise, pick the most clever of your ideas and write a chorus. Once you have reached this point in the exercise, having created a completely unique song based on what was essentially, someone else's idea, then and only then, go back and look up the original song and listen to it. Is there any similarity whatsoever, to the chorus you wrote? I would be willing to bet there is absolutely none. This is why I don't mind sharing ideas, this is why I'm not afraid of ever running out. It's all been done before, just not by you… yet.

If you are not writing these ideas and these moments down daily as they occur, you are letting solid gold pass you by. You have to reach out and grab every little idea and put it in a safe place. A quick scroll through my cell phone will reveal literally thousands of "notes" and entries which each contain either a complete lyric or just a *seed*. A quick scroll through my voice memos will reveal hundreds and hundreds of audio *seeds* any one of which I may decide to work through to completion at any moment of my choosing. Often, I will pull out my cell phone and scroll through my notes which contain seemingly "endless" entries to demonstrate to a student what she must begin to build. My advice, do not ever think that an idea will be there in your mind later. If you have an idea, stop and sing it immediately, or write it immediately. Have I ever pulled over to the side of the road, or stopped in the middle of the grocery store to sing a hook idea into my phone? Absolutely my friend! Did people stare? Absolutely! Do you think I cared what anybody thought? Absolutely not! Some things are more important than one's pride.

The idea mill is a numbers game, generally speaking, an idea mill operates something like this: 100 song seeds = 20 songs = 10 good songs = one awesome song. If your brain is generating 100 song seeds per day, you could be writing one potential number one hit per day. The real exciting production comes when you have 10 and 20 and 30 years of experience behind you and those numbers start to change.

Prince, wrote a song a day for like 40 years. He considered it his job, and he got up and went to work every single day and so should you. Now we are not all Prince, but when you get 100 songs behind you, these numbers will drop to something like this: 100 song seeds = 30 songs = 20 good songs = five awesome songs. And when you get 300 songs behind you the numbers look like this: 100 song seeds = 50 songs = 30 good songs = 10 awesome songs. There is no shortcut, if you do the work, the experience will come, and when the experience comes, the product improves… it's the law of the universe.

The ancient Chinese call it Kung Fu which basically refers to a process of mastering a practice or occupation. As you *master* the craft and creative flow of songwriting, you begin to see astonishing results. Prince wrote at least a song per day for nearly 40 years. That's, conservatively speaking, 14,600 songs, a number I'm told is actually a drop in the bucket. When his heirs began to inventory his vault, rumor has it the estimates are much higher. If he spent just four hours per day writing all those years, then he would've logged a staggering 58,400 hours of writing and his mastery level was through the roof. He would've been writing at *Kung Fu* level at 10,000 hours at which point, most likely every single song he wrote was bullet-proof.

I'm no Prince, but I have absolutely no problem writing one song a day. On any given day I may even write as many as three or four. I have easily invested 10,000 hours into my craft as many other songwriters have. Is it easier for some than others to reach that level of mastery? Absolutely it is. We will always have people like my favorite writer Prince, who was able to write hit after hit at the age of 15, but if you go back and listen to his earlier stuff and follow his songwriting journey, you will notice a clear progression of skill and development of talent. You have to take that same road and work hard and consistently at it. If you hoped to find a shortcut to becoming a great songwriter somewhere in this book, this is it. The short cut is actually a long cut. Start logging the hours and the mastery will come and the quality of your work will increase steadily along the way. If you want to get there faster, then good, there's a simple solution… work harder.

Once I choose a seed and begin to write about an idea, I will sometimes write four or five verses as fast I can then write a basic chorus as fast as I can. These are the basic building blocks of the song which my crafty brain can now work with to start building. I suggest writing through the entire song as quickly as you can so that you can get the basic idea down. Some of the parts of the song, or in most cases, most of it will be terrible. That's okay this is merely the *framing* stage.

Have you ever been in a house that was under construction and it just looked like garbage inside with two by fours going every which way and nailed in bundles and stacks here and there throughout the place? You can see clearly through all the stairs and walls and pass through the back of the closet into the next room? This is called the *framing* stage in building. Framing goes up fast and loose. The carpenters can actually frame up an entire home in a day. If you ever get a chance to watch the process, it's fascinating and scary at the same time. Fascinating in that the skeleton actually goes up so unbelievably fast, but scary in that we actually live in homes that go up this fast. Our rational mind thinks, "how can a structure built so quickly and seemingly haphazardly possibly be safe?" But this is simply how it is done.   If the framers had to work within a pinpoint accuracy of tolerance, this process which takes a day or so, would instead take weeks.

Next, once I got the basic framework up, I go through and start moving lines around, playing with rhymes and meter, shuffling thoughts and ideas until I have a decent amount of cohesion to my verses. At this point I concentrate on my chorus, I sing it to myself several times using a "dummy" melody. Just any old thing off the top of my head to get me through the lines. Oftentimes, a great chorus will *insist* upon its melody. That is a good sign, but often the melody must be agonized over later. Once I'm okay with the basic feel of the chorus I look for the lines that are redundant or unnecessary. I leave them in place until I have replacements written for them. Sometimes, I'll write a half dozen replacement lines for one line I consider weak then ask a mentor to read them and pick the ones he or she thinks are the strongest.

This is that part of construction where the cabinet guys come in and put in all the fancy woodwork which covers all the gaps and rough edges that were visible before. The tile guys come in and cover the floors. Carpet and hardwood goes down and drywall covers up every other imperfection on the walls.

Once I have a great chorus ironed out, I then go back to the verses. Most times, the verses are weak once the chorus is finished and I will then begin to tear each line apart and rebuild it meticulously until the verses clearly support the chorus in a cogent and intelligent way. Not a single syllable can be wasted during this process. I will often go back through the song over and over for a few weeks before I declare it officially finished. I usually resist the temptation to demo the song with more than a guitar vocal (GV) until I have "lived with it" for a few weeks. Just yesterday, I re-wrote a line that has been bothering me on a song for over two years. I've sang the song over and over, mulling it over in my mind, suddenly the other day the idea just popped into my head. I have no idea why it took so long, but now the solution seems obvious. That song is finally finished.   There is no absolute time frame for finishing a song. Some take hours while others take days, weeks, or months. Sometimes it's one word in a song that eats at you every time you hear it for the rest of your life, that doesn't mean it's a bad song. Merle Haggard hates doing *Okie from Muskogee* and its one of his biggest hits. As artists, we have to do our best and strive for perfection while understanding that it can never be fully achieved. At some point, you have to just move on to the next song, painting, story, film, etcetera. And that is okay. If you obsess over every detail so much that you never let the song go out into the world and be a song, you never really grow. Just understand this, a song doesn't have to be perfect to be a hit, but it does have to be heard.

In order to harness the full power of your creative potential, you have to be ever-aware of the ideas that are coming at you all day-every day. When those ideas happen, you cannot judge them, only record them. Become a relentless recorder of the ideas life throws your way constantly, and you will create a backlog that will become more and more like the seed silo mentioned previously.

To see things in the seed, that is genius

—Lao Tzu

Secret # 12

Eat Like A Genius

It has been said by someone wiser than me that if we are not growing, we are dying. If we are not actively getting better, we are by default, getting worse. Visualize yourself in a canoe paddling upstream. What happens if you stop paddling? You start to go backwards down the stream.   If this had been an actual river, depending upon the conditions, this could actually have led to a capsized canoe and possibly injury or death. This is a pretty fair analogy for the importance of maintaining our health. You have to actively contribute to your own health maintenance or suffer the consequences. Is it possible to eat garbage, live like a pig, never go to the doctor and basically spend your life polluting your body, mind and spirit and still be creative? Yes, but what would be the point? Why would you not choose life over death?   Health over sickness? Wisdom over foolishness? Education over ignorance? This book is about hacking into the very best version of the creative genius, and as much as you might want to ignore this chapter, here comes the tough love again... A finely tuned, healthy body is an essential element to peak performance. You cannot work at world class level while mired in a junk food fog. If you are committed to doing absolutely everything you can to improve your creativity, read on.

If you have a tendency to become discouraged concerning diet and fitness, skip this chapter, try the other strategies I've outlined in this book in earnest, and when you are convinced that they work as advertised, which they will... Then come back and re-read this chapter. You may need some other victories under your belt before tackling your health. If you are already in peak health, good for you, but read on anyway. You may actually find some strategies that will help you tune in your body to your creative brain at an even higher level.

In America the vast majority of us have instant access to tons of education, the best healthcare available, and the best food and medicines/nutrition available in the entire world, and yet we perish for lack of all of the above. We have the highest rates of obesity, diabetes, heart disease and cancer in the entire world. We smoke and drink and do drugs and we pass on the legacy of all our destructive habits, pain, and depression on to our children as if it were the inevitable result of progress. It's absolutely insane how unhealthy we are. As a therapist I see it each and every day. People in every corner of America live with awful health, despairing that they are not able to mitigate their bad habits and turn their lives around. Many of us are hopelessly addicted to the foods that are killing us and destroying our creativity and subsequently our productivity.

Steve switches from coffee to beer at eleven am and eats fast food every day. He doesn't even know where a gym is located, and it wouldn't matter if he did because he doesn't have the energy to go there, let alone work out. It is no wonder he writes no more than a half dozen mediocre songs per year, he has barely enough energy to drag himself up off the floor every morning, seldom showers, and smokes a pack and a half of cigarettes a day. For Steve's sake, I wish I were exaggerating. Don't be a Steve.

Elite athletes feed their bodies elite food. Same goes for elite entertainers. When I was on the road with my band, I often rubbed elbows with other entertainers and their crews and got to personally observe how they lived. On their first headlining tour, I was invited backstage to eat dinner with the Dixie Chicks' crew. It was like eating at a five star restaurant only there were vegetarian selections available as well. It was like a traveling health food buffet, literally. I have seen other entertainer's setups as well, most are not quite so elaborate, but the most successful acts know and understand that good food is the cornerstone of a good performance and it shows more than ever, when they are out on the road. I have a family member who is an elite athlete. We were discussing diet the other day and she explained to me that she actually monitors her diet down to the very gram in order to keep herself in peak performance before a meet, now that is some serious self discipline even for a bodybuilder.

Feed yourself like an elite athlete

You are no different. You are an elite in your field. You are the creative genius and you owe it to yourself as well as those who love and depend upon you to tune in to your body and give it what it needs to operate at its very best. This absolutely applies to you. It's not just about self-discipline, if you feed your body properly, your body will take care of you. There are not many guarantees in life, but one thing I feel confident guaranteeing you based on my personal experience is this... If you will employ some self discipline in your diet and exercise habits, your health will improve exponentially, your energy levels will rise, and your creativity will absolutely soar.

There is no one diet that is for everyone, but there are certain common foods which are bad for everyone. I'm just going to bluntly tell it like it is for the rest of this chapter. If diet and exercise is a sticking point for you, or if there are some things that you just don't have the discipline to do consistently, just do what you can. Make a few small changes here and there as you can tolerate them and keep making adjustments as you go along. So let's be realistic... choose your battles, make whatever positive changes you can, and as you see results, implement more strategies. The more results you see from the strategies you implement, the more enthusiasm for positive change you will generate in your life.

Refined carbohydrates are, in my opinion, the number one threat to health in the world. If you could make just one change in your diet that would pay dividends for the rest of your life, it would be to completely eliminate simple carbs as if they were cyanide. I'm talking about sugars like sucrose, fructose and even dextrose, and refined grains like wheat and corn flours. I've seen in my practice, many patients make an enormous difference in their relative health just by making this one simple diet change.   I've seen many patients decrease their blood pressure and cholesterol to healthy levels just by making this one change. It is possible to get off of your prescription medications just by making this simple diet change, but don't take my word for it. Your doctor will tell you the same. Carbs are killing you. So if you want to head off a laundry list of health problems, cut out soda pop, juices, cookies, cakes, most deserts, all processed foods, pizza, pastas, processed yogurt cups, candies, breads, chips, pastries and alcoholic beverages.   If I pretty much just excluded your entire diet, congratulations! Your diet is as bad as mine was when I decided to make big changes for my health and general well-being many years ago. If this is you, this is actually good news because this one change will have such an enormous impact on your life.

Since I eliminated the above foods, I cut my body fat way down, lowered my blood pressure, bad cholesterol, and blood sugar. My energy levels have soared, I sleep all night on a regular basis. And I feel like producing almost all the time. If I'm awake, I'm either writing, producing music, practicing an instrument or seeing patients. I just feel like being busy all the time and I love it. I have the energy to get everything I need done and more. I admit, slowing down is a problem some times, but it sure is a good problem to have. So if you don't eat all the fast food listed above, what do you eat? I'm so glad you asked.

I get that question often. People will often look at my personal "don't" list and say, geez that stuff covers 99 percent of my diet and they feel overwhelmed. I totally understand that feeling, I felt the same way when I realized that my diet would have to give way to my health problems more than 20 years ago. I made some adjustments, changed my habits and I've never looked back. Once you have experienced the dynamite impact this diet has on your overall health, you will not miss the old ways for long. So here's my "do" list. I eat a high protein diet with practically zero simple carbohydrates. Eat this diet and supercharge your creativity.

Eat to supercharge your creativity

An average day for me looks like this: breakfast - six eggs cooked in a tablespoon of coconut oil and a high protein smoothie consisting of leafy greens, blueberries, juice or coconut milk and usually some sort of brain boosting supplement like MCT oil (one of my personal favorites). I am usually not hungry for lunch, but if I am I will eat a piece of fruit, cheese or steak/chicken. For on the go snacking, I make my own jerky but there are also lots of healthy alternatives including nuts and berries. For dinner I have either steak, chicken, or some kind of fish and a leafy green salad. For a nighttime snack, I will often have another smoothie with fruit if I'm feeling like I want something sweet. Yes you can cheat every now and then, but I don't recommend it because it's so easy to fall back into old habits with food. I have an annual piece of pecan pie over the holidays and I enjoy it every bit as much as you might imagine, but the rest of the year, It's pretty much the diet you see here. My family loves to go out to eat, and when we do I seldom have a problem finding something to order, but I have to ask the waiter to leave the carbs off the plate. In addition to this very simple diet which will kick your brain into high-gear, I recommend trying some of the brain-boosting items on this list below. I will also include my favorite smoothie recipes at the end of this book and on my website which you can download and print out for free. But here are some of the key ingredients which should boost your brain power:

 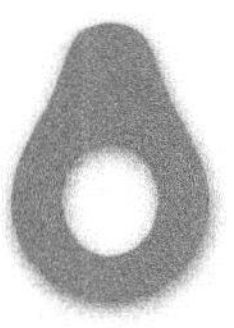 

MCT oil, Collagen Peptides, Coconut, Blueberries, Bilberries, Gogi Berries, Strawberries, Blackberries, Currants, Flax Seed, Chia Seed, Hemp Seed, Almonds, Maca powder, Matcha tea, Guayusa tea (another favorite), Kale, Spinach

These are just a few ingredients that I use more or less, daily in my smoothies. There are a lot of "limitless" pills and supplements out there on the market today also called nootropic supplements. Most of them are extremely expensive, and most of the key nutrients are also found in the above ingredients which I have suggested for your smoothies. Isn't that nice of me? So if you were thinking of taking a supplement, I suggest you try some of these ingredients and see if you are able to get the results you are looking for before trying some expensive pill. Remember, there is no magic pill that is going to make you smarter or more creative or have perfect recall. The purpose of this book is to highlight as many strategies as possible to enhance your abilities. No *one* method is going to have a profound effect on you on its own.   It is the cumulative impact of several of the strategies contained herein which will heighten your productivity and increase your brain power. I'm not saying that each strategy is not going to individually give you great results, I'm just saying that it is the synergistic impact of multiple strategies which will pay you the highest and greatest dividends.

In addition to the diet I suggest above and the questionably delicious smoothies I suggest to you, you may also try any of several teas which may heighten awareness, sharpen your senses, and generally boost your energy and productivity. While most teas and coffees including matcha green tea, and that good old fashioned cup of Joe you may be enjoying each morning each contain a measure of our old friend caffeine, one of my favorite drinks, Guayusa tea, delivers it in a much more consistent manner. I actually listed it above as well, but I think it bears repeating because I believe so strongly in its effects. Whereas most teas and coffees will give you a caffeine buzz that races upwards, followed by a crash, Guayusa tea seems to provide the drinker with a long-lasting sustained caffeine buzz with no crash. It literally feels like, simply more energy; versus that jittery feeling coffee gives you. In south American native culture, hunters will chew the leaves of this plant for days while on hunting trips to provide seemingly unlimited energy while staving off hunger.   In addition to the energy boost, I have personally witnessed near-miraculous anti-inflammatory results.

A few years ago I gave some to a colleague who happens to be a physician. He slugged the entire glass then walked out to see a patient then turned and came back to me and exclaimed, "Doc, I feel it!" I replied, "Oh my gosh, you're standing up straight!" He said, "I know! It healed my spinal stenosis." Of course he was exaggerating, it didn't "heal" it, it just made the inflammation subside for most of the day. We were both pleasantly surprised at this side effect. As far as I know, my friend still drinks Guayusa daily for its anti-inflammatory and pain relieving properties.

Again, one thing that all creative people can and should do to increase brain connectivity is eating right. Let's face it, healthy people in general have better focus and energy.   We feel better emotionally and physically and generally have a better outlook on life.   I find that healthy people are more positive and more likely to make meaningful connections with other people, all of which are great reasons to do it. I've always been of the opinion that eating healthy is its own reward, but there's a good reason why the most successful people in the world are, by and large… the healthiest. So if you want success, eat like a successful person. Go ahead and make the commitment to yourself. Touch your heart and say it out loud…

Tying It All Together

Not every diet is for everyone. We are all unique and it is my intention, only to suggest what has worked for me. If it doesn't work for you, move on and try something else, but let's face facts, eating sugar frosted flakes every morning isn't a healthy long-term solution for anyone. This chapter is about health and discipline, both of which, when optimized, can enhance your creative potential. Try some of these suggestions and see if the results are worth the effort, if not… move on.

I have walked myself into my best thoughts

— <u>Soren Kierkegaard</u>

Secret # 13

Exercise To Achieve Flow

The most successful people in the world exercise like their very livelihoods depend upon it, and personally I think they may be on to something. Some of the most famous thinkers and creators in history were almost fanatical about their exercise routines. For instance, an avid cyclist, Albert Einstein claims to have developed the theory of relativity while riding his bicycle. Charles Dickens walked for hours a day, routinely walking up to 30 miles per day. Beethoven had a similar routine to Dickens. He would rise each morning and work for five or six hours straight, writing constantly, then go out for long walks the rest of the day. Beethoven would take a pen and paper with him on his walks as ideas often came to him while exercising. These walks were so important to Beethoven that he took them every day year round, regardless of the weather. Madonna runs almost every day and when she is on the road, she would setup the day of her show and do a full-length complete rehearsal of her entire show from start to finish.

Have you ever heard someone say, "you're overthinking it." Often, athletes will be accused of choking due to overthinking, but I think the phenomenon is even more prevalent in musicians and entertainers in general. I have personally witnessed this phenomenon many times. The key to getting your performance in any arena up to world class level is to practice both perfectly and obsessively. In excellence, there is no such thing as being over-prepared. No entertainer ever said, "Wow, I wish I would've practiced less."

Have you ever watched an entertainer like Lady Gaga sing and dance simultaneously while playing piano, guitar and bass, standing on her head, doing back flips and cartwheeling into the audience?   Ever wonder how she pulls that off and makes it look like she's just up there peeling a banana? Practice my friend. Pulling off that kind of physical performance, or really any kind of physical performance is to rehearse until you can do each element automatically without even thinking about it. Until you have actually accomplished this task, it is hard to truly understand the freedom that it gives you on stage. People used to ask me why I practiced so hard. While on the road I would spend hours a day sequestered in my hotel room playing the songs in my act over and over again. My band used to tease me saying, "why don't you just practice on stage like everybody else." I did a guitar solo on the acoustic guitar finger-style which had to be absolutely mastered daily or it would not come off automatically. When I was onstage doing this song, people would marvel at how "easy" I made it look. People would shake their heads and say, "how are you able to play that perfectly and still pay the audience your undivided attention?" The secret is, practice until it's automatic. Every single note you play has to be seared into your muscle memory, or it will sound rehearsed. I know this sounds weird, but the trick to sounding natural is to practice until it sounds like you haven't practiced. The great irony is… that's what people see… and they actually believe it. The harder you practice, the more you'll be referred to as a "natural."

"But Doc, why are you off on this tangent about practice?" I'm so glad you asked… If you need to perform, it is important to achieve this "flow" state. It is similar to the flow state where many of your "eureka" moments occur. The key to entering this state is repeating an activity that does not have to be thought about. It is that repetition that drums the mind into creative submission. Often, when I am exercising, I will go into what I can only describe as a trance. Due to previous injuries, I have to do it in a gym on an elliptical, but running is actually one of the most popular sports among creative people throughout the world and throughout history. People often refer to a "runner's high" that occurs after a period of time exercising. Other's describe it as "the zone." However you describe it, the creative genius values this time when the mind enters a relaxed state where the consciousness sort of disconnects with the body and the creative brain goes into overdrive. If you are not exercising to this point several times a week, you are quite likely, missing out on mining this valuable vein of creative ore which exists in all of us. Sometimes while practicing in the zone I will suddenly get a burst of creativity that will lead to a great idea. I often get these bursts of creativity during both practice and exercise.   So, it is critical for you to achieve the "flow" state in order to maximize your creativity. You can achieve it through practice or through exercise.

Flow = breakthrough

All truly great thoughts are conceived by…walking

-Friedrich Nietzsche

Secret #14

Write Bad Songs

Write awful songs, write complete crap if possible. Do you need permission? Here it comes. I give you complete permission to write the worst songs ever written. Now, you have my permission, but let's take it one step forward… Because you should really give *yourself* permission to write bad songs, or paint bad paintings, or whatever it is you do. So touch your heart and repeat after me:

> I give myself permission to
> write bad songs

Anyone who has ever spent anytime in my school has heard me say it a million times. Great songs are not written… they are re-written. This concept is so very important that it bears repeating:

> Great songs are not written,
> they are re-written

If you are afraid to write something poorly, you are very likely to write nothing. This is a fact of writing which any professional will be happy to reiterate for you. I have some great news for you, we all start out writing crap. All first drafts are crap, but without a first draft, there can be no second draft. When I am writing a first draft, I write at high speed. I know it's going to be crap, so I don't stop and dwell on it during the process. I speed-write through the entire song or prose, then go back and start tweaking the work, looking for inconsistencies, problems, bad lines, bad words. If I think that a song has potential, I might rewrite it for months or even a year before I feel that it's ready to be demo'd. A great song goes through multiple re-writes, multiple critiques, and yet it survives. Because of the speed at which I write first drafts, I can literally sit down and write a song in five minutes. Granted, it's not very good, but no song is good in it's initial draft... so get over yourself and write poorly.

Earnest Hemingway once said, "Write drunk, edit sober." He was an avid fan of the bottle so I am told, but he gives us a solid bit of advice here if you just take a moment to dissect it. I like to think literally, drinking while writing was part of his process. I'm not saying that you should get drunk when you are writing, but whatever you do to get into a relaxed state where you can just "zone out" and flow, you should do it, but no, the more important take away from this quote is the "edit sober" part. First of all, it assumes that there is an editing process, but it also assumes that the editing process is far more important than the actual writing process. As I stated before about great songs. Great writing in general, involves a "sloppy copy" stage followed by a meticulous series of re-writes which eventually leads to a great and awesome finished product.

I used to be a big fan of a popular suspense author. For years I waited for each of his books to come out so I could buy them in hardcover and read them before anyone else. But in recent years, his output has gotten so immense that at some point I could no longer keep up. He has basically accomplished this seemingly superhuman feat of writing by two strategies. First, he uses multiple co-writers and mines their efforts. Secondly, he uses a staff of copy-editors so immense that he essentially no longer has to actually do the re-writes himself. It must be nice to reach a stage in your career that you can literally outsource all but the most creative parts of the process. As songwriters, we can't really do that, we have to carry our songs all the way to the finish line even at the highest levels, but the removal of the editing process in the above example, illustrates just how very much time and effort editing adds to the process as a whole.

In my process, I call it "power-writing" because I barrel through the initial draft like a speeding freight train, not stopping to catch my breath or make sure my rhymes are pure. Because of this process, it is not uncommon for me to "power write" up to a half a dozen songs in one day. But only the very best ones get to make it through the editing process. I cull down the ideas until only the best remain to be demo'd. I like to tell people I write lots of bad songs so that I can write that one good one. Don't be afraid to write bad songs. Don't be afraid at all. Write fearlessly… I'll just leave you with this.

> Fear of failure will result in the failure you fear

A man of genius makes no mistakes; his errors are volitional and are the portals of discovery.

-<u>James Joyce</u>

Secret #15

Collaborate

I have been involved in more co-writing sessions than you can shake a stick at, and what often happens is this… There will usually be a writer or writers in the room who are so self conscious about their ideas that they hardly ever speak up during the session. When asked why, they always say the same thing… "I'm afraid what I say won't be any good." The only thing worse than doing the wrong *thing* is doing no-*thing*, and yet that is what we get quite often. Nothing… As a co-writer in a session, it is your responsibility to help keep the session flowing, and this is often accomplished by tossing out idea after idea in a rapid-fire manner until an idea begins to spark and find traction. When that happens, the song then begins to take on more of a solid form and clear direction develops.

Usually a de facto leader emerges in the session and becomes the voice of reason, or sometimes tyranny. This alpha-dog can become very bossy and insistent, actually alienating other writers in the room or in extreme cases, hurting their feelings. Boo hoo. When this happens to you, be a good leader and be kind to others. On the days when you are feeling passive and just don't have the patience to be the leader, then for goodness sake, be a good follower. The only thing worse than a session with a bad leader is a session with bad followers. Once you are well invested in the session and you get to the details of the song, you have too much skin in the song to walk away mad because someone else isn't playing nice. There is a reason why I choose to address this elephant in the Nashville writing room. It is so you can see and recognize it for what it is when it happens to you, because it will. Here is the important thing to remember... We've all been there, just take a breath and roll with it, it ain't about the friendships, it ain't about your feelings, and it certainly ain't about who's in charge. You are in a writing session for one reason, to write, and that is a precious and important undertaking.   And here's the take away... If you are uncomfortable at times during a writing session, good for you!

Allow me to explain... The co-writing session is about stimulating creativity, and in spite of what we would all like to believe, the creation of something wonderful is very uncomfortable, and sometimes it's downright painful. Just ask any woman who's given birth. Some of the greatest songs ever written came from a place of pain, so don't think for a minute that every writing session you enter into has to end with everybody patting each other on the back, tossing back beers and high-fiving.   Often they end in feelings of frustration and disappointment. Sometimes you may even leave a songwriting session with a finished product you don't even like at the moment, but who's genius emerges in the days after.   The empirical evidence behind creativity studies teaches us that this kind of discomfort actually brings out the best in us.   When you are on edge, you are more likely to produce better ideas and better songs, it's the uncomfortable truth. When I'm talking about discomfort, again, I'm not suggesting that you embrace depression or any negative emotion. It is entirely possible to feel negative emotions, benefit from them and yet not respond in a negative way. Some creative people do, but that does not have to be your choice. It is possible to be happy and creative at the same time.

> **Discomfort stimulates creativity**

I absolutely love some of the people I write with, but that is not why I write with them. Often in a writing session, I will be tough on the others in the room. If I feel strongly about an idea, I may just blurt my opinion out. Sometimes, if I'm on the fence about an idea of someone else's, I will challenge the idea just to find out how strongly the other writer feels about the idea, or to probe for rationale. I call it *needling* my co-writers. Look, I think most people would describe me as a very friendly, generous, and good guy. I've been described in a lot of kind ways throughout my life and my career, and I don't mention this to boast. I simply want the reader to understand this concept... You can make-up at the end of the uncomfortable writing session when a great song is in the can.   If you hurt someone's feelings or get your own feelings trampled on during a songwriting session, get thicker skin or find a different line of work. You are not in a session to feel all warm and fuzzy, and if you are feeling nothing but smiles and giggles in a session, beware the quality of the product some of the happiest sessions end with the crappiest of songs.

I don't like being in a session where I'm not being challenged. If I wanted to write unchallenged, I'm perfectly happy doing it alone in my studio. We all know how great we are, we don't need someone else reaffirming our strengths, we need people who don't mind pointing out our weaknesses. You should be writing with people whom you respect enough to to call them on their bullshit if necessary, and whom you respect enough to take notice when their opinions differ from yours, even when it hurts... especially when it hurts. Furthermore, you should be with people whom you are willing to take critique from and still be able to shake their hand at the end of the day and nod and say, yeah, that made me a better person... writer... it's all the same.

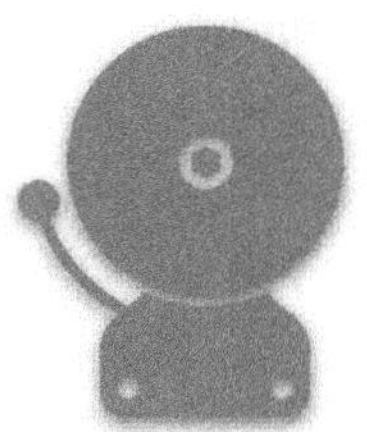

Some people look at a writing session like a tea party. I see it more as a sparring session. I love boxing, but it's not watching the fight that appeals to me most. It's the lifestyle. It's the discipline. I really like watching all the backstory, the training and the sparring before the fight actually airs. To me it is the six months of intense training that leads up to the fight that fascinates me most. Specifically, the sparring is what blows my mind. It's hard enough to punch a bag a thousand times a day, (if you don't believe me, try it). But getting into the ring with a guy who's job is to do his very best to punch you in the face day after day for weeks on end? That is insane. Think of it, the toughest guys in the world hire some of the other toughest guys in the world to try their best to punch them… And they pay them very well. Can you see what I'm getting at? Those guys don't step into the ring with a bunch of creampuffs to make them feel good about themselves. They spar against the best so they can become the best. There is an old saying. Iron sharpens iron.

Iron sharpens iron

Folks who show up to a songwriting session with the good ole boys to be stroked and complimented are ridiculous. I've been in multiple sessions with the proverbial "Mr. Big Time" who opens his conversation like a round of *Six Degrees of Kevin Bacon* describing finally how he was in the room 12 years ago when a song was written that earned a spot as a deep album cut on some guys record whom you've never heard of, but since the album charted, we have to treat the guy like we've been touched by the almighty just by being in his presence. Ever been in that session? The one with the guy who we have to revere because he was the eighth co-writer on an Oak Ridge Boys cut thirty-five years ago. I've been in this session where the guy throws out garbage idea after garbage idea after smarmy cliche' like its pure originality falling from the mouth of angels, and everyone in the room just ate it up like it was manna from heaven. I came out of a session like this once, and literally was tempted to take my copy of the session and toss it in the trash can on my way out the door. Sadly, I actually still have it. A bit of advice, keep everything! You never know when you may have to fight for your co-writer rights!

If you are in a writing session, even if you throw out bad ideas, the bad ideas you throw out may actually make someone else's brain spark something entirely different and unique. In this way, you may actually help write a song that could've never been written without your input, and yet you never actually contributed a solid line to it. And you know what? That's okay... I used to have a cowriter who always seemed to be self-conscious about how much "input" he had with the songs we wrote together. It's not the amount of input that you have in a song that makes you a competent co-writer. Sometimes your competence can be measured by looking at a lyric and leaving it alone because its good just the way it is. Sometimes your contribution may be adding a twist to the melody that makes the song better. Your contribution may be big or small. It may be lyric or melody alone that you contribute, but the term co-writer implies a partnership that is agreed upon when the song is created. Or, at least it is in my studio.

It's always best to have a short conversation about the terms of a writing session before you begin. The vast majority of writers split songs into equal shares with very few exceptions and if great songs are being produced from the partnership, that is all that really matters. If both parties agree on the terms, just let it be. One of my co-writers tells a story about a session with a very famous songwriter. She said after each line was written he would place a number in the margin of the page, which she didn't understand. At the end of the session he added the numbers up and divided by the number of lines in the song and declared that he had written 72% of the song and asked everyone to sign the page to acknowledge this fact. What a jack-ass. She checked around with some other writers and apparently, he pulled this at every songwriting session and people let him get away with it because he was famous. What he obviously didn't appreciate was that his great ideas had most likely arisen from other ideas being thrown around in the session. You can't separate the line from the idea that it came from, and you can't separate that idea from the worse idea that *it* came from. Writing is a partnership wherein trust is required. If you don't respect your co-writers, get out.

> The worst idea may be the greatest contribution to the session

Remember Steve? Steve's first big hit that I told you about happened after he shared a great idea with a few other writers who then helped him finish the song and that song ended up making him a multi-millionaire. Imagine if he hadn't sought co-writer's input on that song? He could've owned 100 percent of that song till the day he died and never made one red cent from it. But as it happened, he shared it and it sparked the initial success that fueled the next nicotine, alcohol and apathy-filled 30 years or so.

At some point after that initial success, bitterness and greed crept in, and Steve decided he would no longer write with co-writers or help other writers get started in the business. He confided in me that he considered that song to be essentially his idea and his song alone and felt that the other writers on the song made millions of dollars just riding on his coat-tails. As a result of his disconnect from the Nashville co-writing and cooperative scene, he never had another hit. Even though every "major" hit he had under his belt were the product of co-writing partnerships, he firmly believed he didn't need them and was better off on his own. To my knowledge, Steve has never had another hit song.   With no affiliation with either another songwriter or a publishing company, he retains all rights to all of his catalogue and it's likely that he'll die with full ownership of a lot of songs that will never make another cent. Don't be a Steve. The more your spread yourself around, the better your chance for success. But don't take my word for it, touch your heart and repeat it to yourself...

I will seek co-writing experience and learn from each one.

Some of the coolest songs I've ever written on my own actually were born out of co-writing sessions where I threw out an idea and wrote it down, and that idea was then rejected by the group and moved on from. I can't stress this enough. Keep an actual pad of paper or journal with a page on your session notes from each and every songwriting session. Write down the time and who is in the room and write down things that *you* think are important. If you do this, you create a backlog of ideas to write from. A year later, you may flip through those notes and find a gem of an idea that everyone passed on. Guess what, that idea is now yours and yours alone, unless of course you decide to bring it back to a cowriting session... wink wink.

If you toss out an idea that you think is great and get nothing but crickets, don't despair. You may actually throw out the exact same idea to the same writer or writers a month later and it will spark something wonderful.   In short, what is a bad idea today may be a great idea tomorrow, so don't be discouraged if no one likes the ideas you suggest. I've thrown out multiple ideas to co-writers, had them pass on what I thought was a great idea, then they turned around and ask me about it a few days later. Sometimes, just because you think you have a good idea, doesn't mean that your co-writers will initially see the potential greatness that you do. By the same token, don't hold back tossing out ideas that you think are bad, because an idea that you think is complete garbage might actually be the spark that creates a hit song. This actually happened to me once. I threw out an idea that I was literally joking about, and everyone was like… yeah that is genius! They took my bad idea and ran with it and we ended up writing a beautiful song from that session which then inspired other ideas. We wound up eventually writing three more songs in one day following that session which started by me throwing out a "joke" while sitting in a coffee shop. My bad idea ended up being the main hook of the song.

I enjoy reading stories about how songs were created. One of my favorite guys in the music business is a guy named Brian Eno. Brian Eno has actually co-written or contributed to some of the most memorable and creative music of our time.   He has worked with legendary artists like U2, Genesis, David Bowie, Talking Heads and many others as a producer and creative *coach* of sorts.   Brian Eno, along with a co-writer named Peter Schmidt, created this "game" which I highly recommend to the creative genius. If you haven't already, you should pick up a deck of "Oblique Strategies" cards. This looks like an ordinary deck of cards, but as a creative genius, this is the greatest card game you will ever play. The whole point of the cards is this, you pick one card out of the deck and do exactly what it says. You cannot pick a card and put it back then pick another card, that would defeat the purpose. You cannot rifle through the cards and pick the strategy that most appeals to you, that would also defeat the purpose. What is the purpose of "Oblique Strategies?" To get you out of your comfort zone. Some of the greatest and most creative hit songs of our time were created as a result of Brian Eno making artists feel uncomfortable in the studio. He sometimes made artists hate him or so I'm told, but his results are undeniably genius, so they always loved him in the end.

The oblique strategies has been described as "the ultimate production tool," and I agree wholeheartedly. Even before I got my copy of the oblique strategies cards, I was already practicing some of them and didn't even know it. My problem however was, and I think we are all guilty of this, we try something new and it works, and we assume that because it works once it will work every time from now on. The reason it worked in the first place was *because* you were trying something new. It is the newness of the strategy that made it work so well, not necessarily the strategy itself. That is not to say you won't get results from the same strategy multiple times, but you will always get better results when you employ a variety of strategies versus just a few of your favorites. When you find yourself in a creative rut, you should really try and shake things up a bit.

One of my favorite stories is of the collaboration between Mutt Lang and Joe Elliot on the Def Leppard hit, "Pour Some Sugar On Me." While this story doesn't specifically involve Eno, it does give us a great example straight out of the *Oblique Strategies* play book. The band recorded the basic tracks to the song which was essentially a "jam" session. Then Mutt and Joe each went into separate sound booths and sang gibberish and random words off the top of their heads into the microphones, then listened to each others' gibberish recordings and wrote down the lyrics which they *thought* the other person was singing. The result is one of the biggest hit records of my entire childhood, and one of the greatest stories of creative genius in rock and roll history.

Okay, over the years I have used some pretty weird strategies to shake up things in my studio, they may not be as unusual as Brian Eno's, but they have worked for me off and on for the last twenty years or so, and mostly on. Sometimes the things you do that make you look like a weirdo, also make you a genius. Some of these are bizarre, but I'm just going to practice what I preach here and throw them out there. You can laugh at me if you want, just know, I'm laughing with you.

Here is a short list of my greatest hits to shock yourself out of a creative slump:

*   Stop what you're doing randomly, go outside and run around your house three times shouting "I'm a genius."

*   Climb up on top of your desk and pose like superman/wonder woman for like five minutes straight. Be totally serious…

*   Do 50 pushups while repeating your favorite affirmations to yourself on each rep

*   Set a timer and play a game for five minutes, careful not to get sucked into a marathon session

* Turn on a recording of a Fugue and sing along with a completely determined look on your face

* Take an ice cold shower in the middle of a creative session

* Roll the dice then slap yourself that many times

* Turn your guitar around and strum with your fretting hand and vice-versa till an idea strikes

* Pick up an instrument you've never played before and mess around with it till you come up with a unique melody

* Get into your car in the middle of the night and go to an empty parking lot and do donuts

* Go to a bookstore to any random section and scan every book title until you've sparked ten song or lyric ideas

* Look in the mirror for five minutes straight while practicing your smile

* Go to a garage sale and just stand around talking to the people till they give you an idea for a song

There are literally a million and a half ways to shock yourself, but this last one is one of my favorites and I do it all the time. So I'm going to give you an example of how to take this idea and run with it. The reason I like doing this is because personally, I think conversation is one of the best ways to spark a song idea, and having random conversations about random topics and family situations with a wide variety of people is very difficult to do, especially if you are the shy type. I mean, who walks up to random people at the grocery store and strikes up a conversation? Not many of us. People always seem to be in a hurry. But if you are at a garage sale, you have been invited to this stranger's home. Their guard is down and they want to be friendly to you so you will buy something. Also, I've found people to be very eager to talk about themselves in general. You just start asking them about their stuff and the memories associated with it, and the next thing you know they're telling you how their grandmother met their grandfather or some other personal story. Sometimes, I will construct a prompt and go to as many garage sales as I can, asking the owner the same question each time, and write down my impressions after I return to my car. You will have the opportunity to have a dozen conversations a day with all kinds of people. It's like having a license to be weird with strangers. There is literally no other social situation I can think of where you are allowed to approach strangers and ask them random personal questions without feeling like you're imposing upon them. Especially not on a hot summer Saturday morning. Sometimes I'll come home from a garage sale session with twenty new song ideas. So try it, you may even find a bargain along the way... What could possibly be wrong with that?

The distance between insanity and genius is measured only by success.

<u>-Bruce Feirstein</u>

Secret #16

Work While You Rest

I touched on this concept earlier, but I will expand on it a bit more here because I believe it is an important point that many of us miss the boat on and many others of us think that it doesn't apply to us. Sleep is an integral element of creativity. If you do not get enough rest, your work product will suffer. It is quite simple, a heathy lifestyle includes rest and without it there can be no balance.

Imagine writing a song without using rests. It would be impossible. It's difficult even to conceptualize it. Yet many of us attempt to live without it. We have all been told that we need a certain amount of rest in order to produce at high efficiency and maintain good physical and mental health. Yet, oftentimes rest is the first element of your health that goes out the window when hard times strike. We all need seven to nine hours of sleep per day in order to keep our sanity, literally. Complete sleep deprivation can lead to acute psychosis within a few days in which an average person may become legally insane and capable of dangerous behaviors and long-term sleep deprivation can lead to all sorts of other mental problems including psychosis, depression, suicide, and stupidity. Okay, just kidding on that last one. But all kidding aside, there are loads of studies out there concerning the human's need for rest and sleep in order to function but even a cursory review of the literature on the subject reveals that sleep deprivation causes people to work slower, with less efficiency and make more mistakes. For songwriters, that means more studio time to complete tasks. And we all know, time is money. Let me put it this way, would you rather be paying session players who show up well-rested and can knock out killer one-take demos for the entire session, or would you rather have guys who've been out all night drinking? However you answered, do likewise. Treat yourself the way you would treat any other studio musician or professional you might hire to do a job. Why would you ever expect any less of yourself than you expect from others?

We all like to hear the stories of creative geniuses who worked for days on end and only took cat naps in their laboratories and that's all well and good because they are merely **stories**. I have a theory about this and I'm going to share it here and now. Some people are not going to like this very much but if you don't, you can mark a big X through this section of the book, after all it's your book…

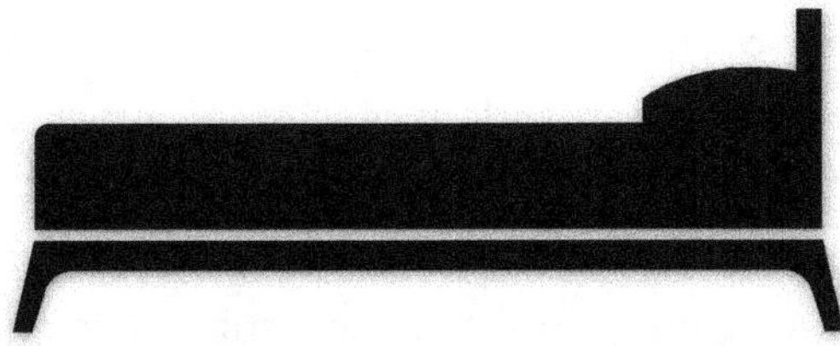

I think those stories of creative geniuses who stay up for days on end and never slept are, for the most part, a load of crap. As a species, humans have a tendency to classify the genius as having some qualities that we ourselves do not possess. It is important to dispel all of these myths so as to remove all possible barriers to your success. The ability to stay up for days and work does not make you a genius, if that were the case, Hitler was a genius but he was also a methamphetamine addict, so there's some food for thought. If you follow the logic as it applies to the collective psyche, it goes like this. Geniuses are people who can stay awake for days and work uninterrupted in order to make magical things happen, therefore I must not be one since I cannot do the same. In other words, people have a tendency to attribute super-human qualities to the genius so they can comfort themselves for not being one. This is another example of the human mind's uncanny ability to bullshit itself into believing it's okay to be mediocre. *There there, you may as well quit, after all, successful people posses a trait that you cannot ever aspire to.* Geez, what a load of crap. You are fully capable of accomplishing the work of the creative genius. No one is holding you back but you.

You are fully capable of accomplishing the work of the creative genius

When you hear of some crazy story of someone you admire performing some super-human feat of sleep deprivation, take it with a grain of salt. Some of that stuff is made up nonsense and legend, and while the achievements of the creative elite are amazing, they are still humans for the most part, and therefore subject to the same laws of nature as the rest of us. They all had to have their beauty sleep. Personally, I get six to seven hours of sleep per night and I love me some nap time in the afternoon. Sometimes when I'm out and about, I'll just pull over my car when I feel the urge and take a quick twenty-minute nap. It's awesome! If you are feeling tired or drowsy, think to yourself… *"what would it hurt to just stop and sleep for a bit?"*

Another important element of sleep, and the reason we all need it is, it puts our brains into that wonderful and blissful "alpha" state followed by the even better, "theta" state where REM sleep occurs. I touched on the idea earlier that we can task our subconscious to work on problems for us, effectively using it like an assistant. Try this the next time you take a nap or go down for the night. Think of a project or song you are working on, sing your way through it until you get to the part you are stuck on, then literally instruct your brain to work on that part of the song while you are asleep. Concentrate on the problem area as you drift away to sleepy-land. Oftentimes, when I do this little exercises, I will awake with the answer. The line will just pop into my head, the melody will just *be there* the next time I go through the problem area. I already touched on placing ourselves in "alpha" several times a day. This is nothing more than a deeper form of relaxation than most people enjoy throughout the day, but when you extend your naps to over 45 minutes, you invite the much deeper "theta" state. You actually allow yourself to go through an entire REM cycle during a longer nap. Experiment with naps and longer rest periods and find some strategies that keep your brain solving problems for you twenty four hours a day. Your brain will thank you. Touch your heart and say it with me.

Further evidence exists in the area of the subconscious mind's ability to solve problems and create for us while we sleep. There are many examples of this phenomenon, but I will just share a few. Keith Richards wrote the song *Satisfaction* after hearing it in a dream. Paul McCartney wrote the song *Let it Be* after hearing his mother say it in to him in a dream. Other examples include, *Purple Haze*, *Yesterday* and the list just goes on and on. The jury is in, I shouldn't have to further convince you that your brain never stops its wonderful work. The workshop elves are in there slaving away for you. It's just that through most of your conscious down time it's busy putting a sweater vest on a giant squid and playing backgammon with him while cooking hotdogs over an open ice fire with your third grade math teacher. The mind's ability to recall and make strange, curious and wonderful connections is never more obvious than when we are dreaming. So dream with purpose.

> ## Dream with purpose

Now, I'm not going to tell you your sleepy-time is going to suddenly become a tiny little song writing factory over night, and I'm not saying I wake up every single morning with a hit song. This is just one of many strategies for you to work on in order to spark your creative genius. With a little effort, you can actually become the "conductor" of the madness that occurs in your dreams to some small degree. For instance, I already described how I direct my subconscious while I am drifting off and it often obeys me. I think I've either gotten better at it over the years, or I've just become more acutely aware. For instance, I have often had what I would call *lucid dreams* which is simply the term for being aware during the dream that you are indeed, dreaming. You can achieve this state by meditating as you drift off. Just concentrate and say to yourself, I am going to be fully aware that I am dreaming tonight, I am going to enter my dreams as an observer and come back in the morning with a beautiful and creative gift from my subconscious mind. The feeling of lucid dreaming can be strange if you have never experienced it, but most of us have experienced the phenomenon on some level if only as children.

During REM sleep, our bodies go into a state know as *sleep paralysis*. Sleep paralysis is the mechanism wherein our brains shut off the signals to our bodies so we don't run around like lunatics all night long. Have you ever awoken from a dream where you were fighting and actually bopped your partner in the back? Or have you ever been running in your sleep and awoke to find yourself kicking your legs? These are examples of what happens when we emerge from sleep paralysis suddenly. Have you ever experienced sleep walking? This is a glitch of sorts that occurs when the body doesn't fully enter the state of sleep paralysis. Well, during lucid dreaming, you actually know that you are dreaming, and when you become aware that you cannot move your body, it can be quite unnerving, especially if something very sudden occurs in your dream and you realize that you cannot react. If this happens to you, just remind yourself that you are in a dream and that nothing bad can happen. Try it tonight, and remember to bring back something useful even if its a phrase, a thought, an idea, a feeling, an emotion, or a pain. Enter a restful state expecting to glean some useful work product from that six to eight hours of unconsciousness. Your dreams may be surprisingly productive.

Men of lofty genius when they are
doing the least work are most active.

-Leonardo da Vinci

Secret # 17

Manage Your Time

I think, at least in the United States, we are conditioned to live our lives as if work is the single most important thing to us. It starts when we are children and it never ends. Americans spend more time at work than people of almost any other country. Most of us are obsessed with productivity and I am no exception. If you think I'm about to get on my high horse and lecture you about work/life balance, you have come to the wrong teacher because I struggle with it just as much as any other red-blooded American. But, I am trying to achieve a work/life balance and I think my family appreciates it.

My problem is, I feel like I have to be producing some kind of product constantly. If I let a day go by without either actually earning money or putting intellectual property in the bank, I am really and truly lost for the day. I realized this was a problem last year when I went on vacation and awoke the first day with a serious, stress-related illness that ended up leaving me in excruciating pain throughout my entire vacation. I hadn't realized it, but the stress of taking off from work literally triggered this illness. When this happened, I began to do some serious soul-searching and came to the following conclusion. Balance is not something that happens by accident. As we go through our lives, our interests wax, wane, and surge, and as they do we can gradually get terribly out of balance without even realizing it until it's too late. It is so easy to let any pleasurable interest run away with you. It is the job of the creative genius to actively and consciously create and maintain a healthy balance. Touch your heart and say it with me…

Too much of a good thing is usually a bad thing. Some people like to use this saying to condemn us for our vices, but it actually is quite germane to the present discussion. I used to have an uncle Danny who had some wise and colorful sayings. One of my favorites went like this. The main thing is to keep the main thing the main thing. Uncle Danny was no poet, but on this point, he was right. This principle alone, when applied to the balance equation has a soothing effect. It is great to work and create and produce and change lives, heal people and promote happiness in general, but if you are doing it to the detriment of your relationships, balance is lost. If you think it cannot happen to you, you are already in danger. So take some advice from Danny and keep your priorities straight.

I know a guy who works two full time jobs simultaneously. He has eight children and he is the soul breadwinner. He literally gets up at five o'clock every morning and heads off to work at a factory from six am to two-thirty, then drives directly to another job that starts at three o'clock, gets off at eleven and heads back home for a nice restful four or five hours of sleep. He has a nice big home and drives a pretty car, but he has no time to be with his family or enjoy all the stuff he's working for. The sad part which he probably won't realize for many years is this... His children will never even appreciate the sacrifices he's made for them to dress nice and live in a fancy house. In the end, they will simply resent him for not being around. They will call him a workaholic and curse their luck at being stuck with such a terrible absentee of a father. What's more, the guy's wife is so starved for adult attention that she spends most of her leisure time with her own friends. Basically, they are a married couple who live completely separate lives. They hardly know each other and it's only going to get worse. The problem is, no balance.

Your life is an hourglass

Like I said before, this is not been my strong suit for the last twenty years or so, but over the past few years I have really buckled down and begun to manage my time better and better and it has helped to manage it in the same ways that I manage other areas of my life. Most people manage, or I should say... *mismanage* their time as if it were an infinite resource.   This is a foolish practice. You have a very finite amount of time in your life and the sooner you really settle yourself into that fact, the sooner you will start to get things done. Your life is not a stopwatch, forever rolling forward. It is an hourglass. You have no clue how much sand it contains.

Since time is money, shouldn't you manage your time as wisely as you manage your money?   If you want to get things done without neglecting the most important of them all, you have to compartmentalize. One of the most popular and effective budgeting strategies is the envelope method. We've all probably heard of it, but I will briefly explain. This is a budgeting strategy wherein money is divided into envelopes at the beginning of the month according to each purpose for which it is intended, and when the money in the envelopes is gone, you're done spending for the month. It's pretty simple and very effective if you have the discipline to stick with it. We can use a similar method to budget our time, and if you do this with some discipline, you will find it to be just as an effective strategy with time as it is with money. The only difference is, we do it by the day. First, do this… make a list of all the things that you have to get done in an average day and place an amount of time out next to it. Once you get your list made and you're pretty sure it's all on there, make a new list on a separate sheet of paper, transposing the first list in order of importance. Once you get that list made, it might look something like mine here:

Activity	Time in hours
Family time	2
Write	4
Sleep	7
See patients	7
Meditate	.5
Travel	.5
Grooming	.5
Eating	1.5
Exercise	1
Total	24

This is an average week day for me. Yours will probably look similar. Sometimes I get off a bit, but basically I know that if I have been writing for 6 hours, my wife is getting lonely in the other room, my children are feeling neglected, or I'm not going to be sleeping very much tonight. There is no way to force more hours into your day. No matter how much you try. That's why there's so much hype about multitasking. It is a pop-culture *catch phrase* tossed about to try and solve the above time problem, but it is unfortunately been scientifically proven to be a fairy tale. No matter what you do, you are left with only 24 hours in your day, and from a scientifically sound perspective, if you are attempting to multi-task, you are actually taking more time to complete the tasks than you would be if you were focusing on them individually.

So you have the envelopes above to consider when you wake up in the morning. Any *time* you remove from one must be stolen from another. In my life as you see it above, the exercise envelope is the first casualty. That's why its on the end. If I get my exercise 3 days a week, I have achieved balance. For this to work like a real budget, you have to place the envelops in the order of their importance to you, *not* in the order of how much time they are allotted. For instance, writing is one of my priorities, so it's near the top of the list even though it doesn't get as much time as my sleep. Now the final step... perform each with discipline and focus giving the most importance to the ones at the top of the list. Let the bottom of the list suffer first if your day becomes shortened.

Other songwriters often look at this list and they can't believe I actually spend 4 hours a day writing in my studio every day and sometimes as many as 12 hours a day on the weekends. My response usually goes like this… is writing important to you? If it is as important as you say it is, you will spend time doing it every day. There is an old saying you've probably heard in church. It goes something like this… where a man's treasure is, there will his heart be. This is an important point I make here because if you are a writer, a creator of art, a builder of buildings, or a designer of any and all things beautiful, your time is your treasure and your art is your heart.

I have gone to many songwriter meetings and discussion groups and sat down with many songwriters to prepare to write this book, and I am often perplexed when I find out how very little time other writers actually spend working on their craft, if you are lucky enough to be able to afford to write full-time, you have my unwavering envy because I love it so very much that I feel I could do it all day every day and never run out of enthusiasm for it, but if you are a part time writer, you really have to struggle to make time for it. If you don't make time for the things you are the most passionate about, what in the world are you living for? Pick the things that mean the most to you and do them first every single day of your life and your happiness level will soar.

There is no genius in life like the genius of energy and industry.

—<u>Donald G. Mitchell</u>

Secret #18

Be Tenacious

One of the most important tenets to the creed of the creative genius is tenacity. Personally, I believe this is the most important of them all. I could write an entire book on this single word. It can further be defined as grit, backbone, fortitude, guts, spunk, pluck, determination, purposefulness, nerve, endurance, and long-suffering. If you want guaranteed success in life, the road is paved with hard work and the ditches are littered with the bodies of the quitters.

Early in my career I sat down and tossed back a few too many drinks with the legendary songwriter, Wayne Carson (*You were Always On My Mind*). I asked him a lot of questions as you might imagine, and he was more and more gracious and kind as the bar tab grew. At one point I asked him the same generic question I've asked many famous songwriters over the years; "What is the best advice you can give me as a songwriter?" He took a long pull off his Budweiser longneck and sat it down and looked at me and said, "Well son... no one ever made it big *after* quitting."

This guy is arguably one of the most successful songwriters of all time and his number one nugget of wisdom was all about grit. I asked the same question when I met with Willie Nelson a few years back, and his advice was, "Just keep writing Doc, the hits'll come." I had the pleasure of asking this question of "Whispering Bill Anderson" once and he said, "You never know where your next hit is coming from." I'm actually not sure he understood the question. Anyway, Tommy Barnes,

Kenny Beard, Wild Bill Emerson, Tommy Overstreet, David Stewart, MaryLou Turner, even our friend Steve... Literally every great songwriter, artist, and entertainer I've ever sat down with all have the exact same advice. "Don't give up."

The point is, tenacity eventually wins. Tenacity eventually gets what it wants.   Tenacity holds on after everyone else has let go.   Tenacity cannot be overcome, it has to be either satisfied or killed. So what do you want? Once you have answered that question, set your goals, let tenacity take the wheel, and never ever, ever give up.   Never stop growing, never stop learning, never stop putting yourself in the way of success, and eventually it will hit you.

I had a great friend when I was in college who was also one of my first guitar students. His name was Jeremy Wise. Jeremy was an awesome guy, a ferocious competitor and a fast learner. It didn't take long for me to teach him everything I knew at the time about guitar, but he taught me something even better. I was in the Army National Guard at the time and Jeremy, a few years my junior was a great workout partner. He sort of looked up to me at the time and it felt good to encourage him in music and in military service. I remember running with him for five or six miles in the Arkansas heat and I could be ready to quit about a hundred times over. I would look over at Jeremy and he just appeared to be possessed. He simply didn't have that switch in his head that ever told him that it was time to quit. He was an amazing person. Anytime I've been in a physically demanding situation over the years I always imagine that crazy kid looking at me like, *"so when does this get hard?"*

Jeremy later went on to become a Special Operator in the US Navy Seals and served most of his career in the middle east, but one of the most curious and amazing things about Jeremy's career as a special operator was how it started. Everyone has heard of BUDS training, which is basically where the toughest men in the world go to see if they have what it takes to become a Navy Seal. Jeremy made it almost all the way through BUDS, the most grueling elite military selection process in the world, when he suffered an injury that put him in the hospital and out of training. For most guys, that would have been the end of his career. If you are recycled, you are out. This is simply the way it has always been for the would-be special operator, but not Jeremy. As soon as he was able, he went back and pleaded relentlessly to be allowed to start over, and after weeks of begging, he was allowed to recycle. To the best of my knowledge he remains the one and only man ever to repeat BUDS and succeed to become a SEAL. That's grit. Even among SEALs, Jeremy was a bad-ass of the highest order.

Jeremy, unfortunately was killed in action by a cowardly terrorist strapped with explosives. When I heard that he had died the first thought that ran through my head was… "That's the only way anybody could have ever stopped Jeremy. They had to sneak up on him with a bomb. God help em they ever had given Jeremy a chance to fight back. He has been a lifelong inspiration to me of courage, discipline and grit. Anytime I've ever thought of quitting, I think of Jeremy and I just keep going.

Yes, there are people who have certain qualities that make them outliers in sports. Someone out there is the world's tallest, world's strongest, leanest, skinniest, smartest, richest, etc. But for the most part, we all share the same basic makeup and physicality. Two arms, two legs, one head, if you're lucky, a brain… in other words we all have the same parts and the same basic human needs for nutrition, rest, activity, etc. You are basically no different than any other high creative achiever whom you admire. There is probably no special quality that they possess which you cannot yourself possess with enough work and tenacity. And most importantly, there is no amount of natural talent that you cannot out work. Touch your heart and say it with me.

> There is no amount of natural talent that I cannot out work

One of my favorite movies is "Rudy." If you haven't seen it, I highly recommend you do so because it is so incredibly inspiring. It is the true story of a 5'6", 165 pound kid who had no talent and absolutely no business on a football field, except that he had a dream and refused to be denied. He actually applied to Notre Dame and got rejected three times, and this is after everyone in his life had already told him he couldn't do it. This guy was laughed at, abused, and basically tortured for four years. As an undergraduate he struggled mightily in both class and on the field as basically he was a punching bag for the scout team, which was actually the Notre Dame *practice* team. However, through tenacity, determination, and pure heart, he managed to achieve his goal. After enduring years of hardship, he was allowed to dress for one single game, the final game of his senior year and his last chance to be recognized as an official Notre Dame football player. He played three plays and sacked the quarterback on the last one. Up until that day in 1974, he was the only player in the history of Notre Dame football to ever have been carried off the field by his teammates.

Rudy was a little guy, obviously he was never going to make the NFL right? Well I personally met a 5'6" running back for the Kansas City Chiefs a few years back who didn't weight more than a buck sixty-five. The smaller players have to outwork their larger and more physical counterparts and they understand this. This is just a fact of life. If you want something bad enough you must simply work harder than anyone else to get it. If the perceived obstacles to your dreams are enough to hold you back, then maybe you don't really want them that badly. I'll say it a bit differently: If you can be held back, you will be.

> If you <u>can</u> be held back, you <u>will</u> be

So how does this apply to we, the creative geniuses of the world? We may never be actually carried off the field by our teammates, but if we work long and hard enough and produce enough, we can earn a good living at it. If it's your side hustle, then good for you. For some of us that is enough, but if your goal is to receive a Grammy, a CMA, an ACM or an Oscar, then you will be needing a clear understanding of tenacity. If you want to attend your own #1 hit party on music row, you will need a healthy dose of grit. If you want to have a song at number one on iTunes, you will need more perseverance than the next person. Doing the right thing is important, doing all the right things is even more important, doing all the right things longer and harder than anyone else is your ticket to having lived an exceptional life. If your bucket list involves achieving greatness, then you need to grab hold of this concept like a bulldog and lock your jaws around it and never, ever let anybody shake you off of your dreams. Touch your heart and say it with me…

I am incapable of quitting

We can all be geniuses because one definition of genius is the infinite capacity for taking pains.

<u>-Knute Rockne</u>

Secret # 19

Procrastinate!

Now, I'm going to sound like a hypocrite here because I'm not a big procrastinator, but there are times when procrastination has resulted in enhanced creativity. Procrastination is just another tool in your bag of tricks as a creative, and it can actually be a powerful one. Allow me to explain...

In school, maybe you were one of those people who would put off that ten page paper till the night before it was due then stay up till five in the morning doing a half-assed job on it. I know, the struggle is real. Fortunately, that was never me. I was always the geek who asked if I could get extra credit for turning it in early. I would have nightmares about not getting papers done in time or finding out with one week left to graduate that I had forgotten to show up to one of my classes for the entire semester and would have to repeat the program. This is actually stifling in a way and I actually had to overcome it to become more creative. People like me have a lot of difficulty "letting go," and endure through life in a state of perpetual anxiety about getting things done. And as we all know, anxiety is not really a good thing. It's not healthy to our bodies or minds, and it can contribute to a lot of chronic illnesses if allowed to go uncontrolled.

Part of my journey as a seeker of my own creative genius has been learning to "let go" and allow myself to procrastinate projects. For this reason, my personal workflow involves having multiple projects going at once and going back and forth from project to project in order to let my mind rest and "percolate" on multiple ideas at once. Remember when I said multitasking is a bad idea? Let me make this distinction… this is not multitasking. When I am into a project, I focus on it exclusively in that moment, but I don't necessarily stay on that one project until it is completely finished.

As I write these words, I have 13 songs in production on my DAW (digital audio workstation), I have at least 300 partial songs going in my google "Keep" folder, and I have multiple writing projects going with several other artists and songwriters in KC and Nashville and dozens of songs waiting to be demo'd. So, in a way, I'm working on one project while I "procrastinate" on another. If I went through my life waiting to completely finish each project before starting a new one, it would decimate my output. So learn when to let go and move on.

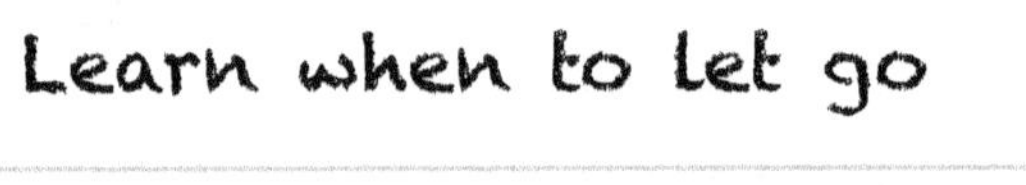

Procrastination can also actually be more literal and deliberate. Earlier in this book, I discussed how the subconscious mind continues to work on your projects and problems long after you have consciously set them aside. This is often an extremely effective strategy that you can use to boost your creativity. If you find yourself running on creative fumes on one project, just shift gears and work on something else for awhile. Once you do this, in a way you have issued a challenge to your subconscious mind which then continues to address the previous project while you are consciously working on the next one. I suggest you also keep a running list that you can review daily to keep the ideas fresh in both your conscious and subconscious. I call this my *circle back* list. Just remember, a brick wall is not really a stopping point, it's just a starting point for a different project. Keep going back to those problems on your "circle back" list and they will all eventually find resolution.

Have you ever noticed that withholding pleasure is sometimes the most effective way to enhance it? Whether its your favorite dessert, affection, sex, a smile, a gift, holding it back and waiting is often just the extra enjoyment that makes it that much more special. Why is a gift that sits under the tree for weeks wrapped in brightly colored paper so much better than the gift that's handed to you in a Wal-Mart bag like a six pack of beer? When you were a kid, do you remember that one family member who shows up late to your birthday party and hands you the gift that they "Didn't have time to wrap?"   Kind of disappointing wasn't it?   It wasn't that the gift is any better or worse than any of the others, it's just the anticipation is missing. Well, you can use the same strategy to force your mind to do fireworks and back flips as it anticipates the big finish which it knows is coming.   Your subconscious mind is like a show-off kid that is dying to impress you.

Try the following strategy the next time you get flummoxed on a particularly difficult project that you're desperate to finish. Pull out a random book and read a chapter. You will want to stop reading and get back to the project, resist the urge.   Instead, pull out your cell phone and go through all those emails, your mind will try to pull you back to the project, resist the urge. Go outside and walk around the block, enjoy the breeze, the trees, the birds, the bees, but refuse to think about the project. Your mind will keep pulling you back to it. Resist the urge. Actively procrastinating will drive you crazy with the anticipation of getting back to the project. When you finally "give in" and return to your studio, you may be pleasantly surprised to find the pieces falling into place as if by magic. Active procrastination will often lead to the breakthrough you desire the most. I will say it again...

Active procrastination can effect
the breakthrough you desire

Desperation is sometimes as powerful an inspirer as genius.

<u>-Benjamin Disraeli</u>

Secret #20

Work At Peak Creativity

I am a morning person. There's something about jumping out of bed and running hard at my problems that seems to energize me, so I will focus here on what I know is true for me. If you are a "night" person or an "afternoon" person, good for you! I wish you the joy of it. It is not my intention to absolutely generalize what works for me to everyone else. We are all individuals and what works well for me may only work well for you from midnight to 3 AM. The greater point of this chapter is to find your peak performance hours and exploit those hours to your greatest possible strategic advantage.

Some studies show that, for "morning people," your mental acuity is at its peak for the first two hours after waking up, yet most of us use this amazing mental focus and powerful creative potential to watch TV, surf through social media on their phones and sip coffee, or even worse, waste it on some mundane task like driving to work. Have you ever wondered why most commuters cite the morning commute as being the most frustrating part of their day? Is there any wonder? Your mind is ready for calculus and you're giving it ABC's and if there's traffic, forget about it... you just took a rote task and made it drag by even slower. It's a wonder people ever even make it to work at all.

There is an old saying, early to bed and early to rise makes a man healthy, wealthy and wise. Well, I'm not going to ask you to get up earlier at the expense of a good night's rest. What I am suggesting is that, if you are a morning person... once you are well rested, you should rise from bed, spend a short time in grooming and meditation, grab a quick bite, then work for the next two hours on, you guessed it... your "genius" skill, which for myself is writing. As humans, we are very schedule driven people. We like to go to bed at the same time, get up at the same time, we eat our meals at about the same time every day, etc. But you can actually learn to be the ruler of your own schedule. There is no law that says you have to get up out of bed at the last possible second and rush directly to your day job across town... if like most people, that's what you do.

If you have a day-job you have to get to by say, eight o'clock, then structure your day so that you go to bed two hours earlier, rise two hours earlier and write like mad during those critical first two hours of peak productivity from five till seven. As I discussed earlier, if writing is high priority, you should place it at the time of your day where your performance is at its peak. So, if you are a morning person, you should get your writing in and out of the way first and let the rest of the day fall in line behind it. If you are like me and are committed to writing two to four hours a day, then structure your day accordingly. Get those hours in first thing. If you will commit to trying it for a week, you will be absolutely astonished at the additional product you create in that short period of time. I'll say with conviction that the amount of work you would normally get done in a month will get done in that first week alone. And from there forward, the sky's the limit.

> Prioritize your most important tasks to your peak performance time of day

In recent history many companies have recognized this simple principle of enhancing productivity. This concept has been a critical motivator toward the telecommuting boom that has taken place over the past ten years. The most progressive companies are interested in harnessing your creative potential when it is at its peak and they recognize that it isn't necessarily from nine to five. Furthermore, today there are more entrepreneurs that at any time since the industrial era, and the most successful individuals capitalize on it. This "secret" to success is really no secret. It is ancient wisdom that has enhanced creativity since the beginning of time. You are no exception to the rule. If you want to produce more and with greater creativity, identify your peak performance time of day and prioritize your creative work to coincide with it.

Who makes quick use of the moment is a genius of prudence.

-Johann Kaspar Lavater

Secret # 21

Find A Mentor Be A Mentor

We seem to live in a "do it yourself" society. We feel it all day every day, it has become an integral part of our culture, and I'm not so sure it's a good thing. Okay, I can turn a screwdriver or a wrench, so I don't see the problem with changing a light switch or even replacing a garbage disposal, but when you walk into the store, look around for ten minutes then actually feel guilty for "bothering" an associate to ask for help in finding something? Isn't that a little much? Okay a trip to the store goes something like this… You are expected to go in, find what you need without asking for help (as if you could find someone anyway), then take your purchase to the front of the store, check yourself out, carry your purchase to your car and load it up yourself, even if its a seventy inch television. Salespeople no longer exist. Stores are like self-serve feeding troughs these days. The only time you will get any attention is if you try to walk out without paying.

The same thing happens when we walk into a restaurant, walk up to the counter, order your coffee, pay for it then the barista clears her throat loudly and nods at the tip jar. Tips used to be an exchange for service, and moreover, a higher quality of service demanded a higher quality of tip. Nowadays, the tip is simply expected regardless of the quality of service. Personally, I tip no matter what, but sometimes I really resent it, especially at drive-throughs and buffets. Basically I'm doing the job for the waiter, serving myself for the most part, yet I'm still expected to tip… and I usually do, but I feel like such a rube. I feel as though the service industry wants to have their cake and eat it to. What if you took your car in to get an oil change and the manager just came out and pointed to the bay and said, "Park there and get busy. Let us know when you're finished and place your tips right here, we'll be in here staring at our phones."

The point here is this... our culture has trained us to do everything ourselves and never even ask for help, and that is not just a bad thing, its an awful thing. Furthermore, much of the adult workforce has moved away from apprenticeships and internships. The only ships out there nowadays are *sole-proprietorships* which further exacerbates the "do it yourself" culture. Now don't get me wrong, I am not harkening back to the good old days of sexism, racism, and all the other awful "isms" that the former generation perpetuated, all I'm saying is, we need to know when to ask for help, and we need to understand that its okay. You are not any less of a person for having asked for help.

My wife is a teacher so I see this all the time. So many of her children would rather cheat and copy and paste some random article from the internet than to come to her and ask for help with the assignment. In the age where raw information is free and unlimited for the most part, we have become a generation of cheaters, because the grade is more important than the knowledge. This generation is the unwitting victim of the do-it-yourself culture. Even when I was a child the beast had already begun to take shape. The days of finding an adult who was doing what you wanted to do and simply asking them to teach you how to do it were pretty much over by the time I was a teenager. Now it's long gone, but in a way, the spirit of that time still lives on in each of us. You see, we were all born to teach. Touch your heart and say it with me...

Songwriting is like a trade. We have lots of resources available to us, but there is no better teacher than another human being. Songwriting is a very nuanced craft, but it is a craft nonetheless. The best way to learn a craft is by doing. But the best way to do is by watching and learning with a mentor, by interacting and questioning the source of that knowledge. You can't get that from a podcast or a YouTube video, there is no real Q & A, no dialogue, no feedback, no relationship. Only another human being can really explain how to construct a song. Most people are afraid to ask for help, and in not asking, their talent is never developed properly or fully.

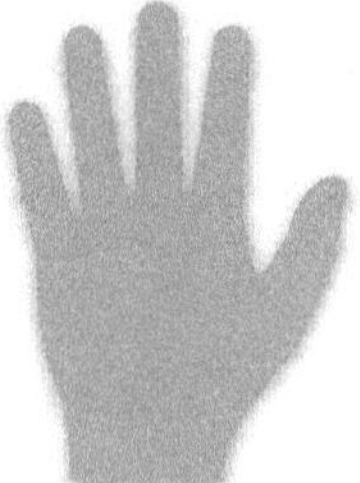

Personally, I have never turned away someone who has asked for a helping hand with music. I think most people will be willing to help you if you are willing to do what they say. That is the key sticking point. I have had many people ask me for help and I say, well here's where you're at and this is what you should do next. Go do it then get back to me and I'll tell you what your next step is. Most often, you never hear from those people again, and that is unfortunate because I am more than willing to take them all the way through the process. I've found that some of the people who ask me for help really are asking for me to do it for them. When they discover the reality that something will be required of them in the process, they suddenly find that they really don't want my help after all. The point is this... a mentor cannot help you if you aren't willing to do what he or she says. If they think enough of you to give you advice, you should think enough of them to take it. If you don't follow through, you obviously don't value the advice.

> **If you value the advice, you must follow through**

Personally, Mentorship has been a very big part of my life. I've had great mentors myself, but I've grown just as much by mentoring others. Over my adult life I have influenced thousands of kids, I've taught hundreds in my school, but I've only truly "mentored" a few dozen, and of those few, I continue to work with even fewer as they continue their journey in the music business. As I watch them go deeper and learn more and more, I'm always waiting and watching, always ready to step in and lend a hand or an ear and to help in absolutely any way that I can, but they have to ask for help. They know there is an open door and all the help in the world that I have to offer, but they must ask. And in so doing, they make my life richer and fuller. This is the beauty of teaching someone else... when you do so, you teach yourself and you grow more than you ever thought you could.

In this chapter I hope to inspire you to do two things: first, to find mentors for yourself, and second, and perhaps more importantly, to find someone who knows less than you and teach them what you know. In so doing, it forces you to take stock in what you do and do not understand while highlighting both your weaknesses and your strengths. When you do this, your confidence will grow in direct proportion to your self-awareness.   Furthermore, as you seek mentorship, be willing to pay for it.

Early in my career I went around Nashville and Branson meeting with every industry insider I could get an appointment or buy coffee or a lunch for, and asked them for help. The overwhelming majority were extremely kind, generous and forthcoming with their good advice. And when they doled it out, I literally wrote it down right in front of them, I went out and did what they said, and then I would write them a thank you note along with feedback about how their advice helped me or changed my life. Some would call this "sucking up" I just call it good manners, and people really and truly appreciated it then, and they still do. If someone cares enough to give of themselves, have the curtesy to show that you appreciate them. Furthermore, there are a lot of good people in and around the music business who's business is all about helping young artists and entertainers find their way in the business. This business is expensive and those experts have to eat just like everyone else. They can't all afford to help you for free, and even if they did, there is a possibility that you would not benefit from it. Read on...

One point where I missed the boat early in my career was when it came to taking a class on songwriting or paying for a workshop or a clinic, I was reluctant to shell out the dough.   I remember this feeling of resentment I would get when someone said, "that'll cost you."   I remember feeling very suspicious of people, especially in Nashville who wanted to "help" me with one hand while sticking the other in my pocket. Boy, was I ever a dope. It took almost losing my voice to change my mind. At one point in my career, I was doing a big mix of studio singing, fairs and festivals, but still singing a lot in bars and clubs around the country. The last year before my injury, I did a total of about two-hundred and sixty shows. In case you are wondering, that's a lot. The last summer I toured, I did over a hundred shows in two months at five consecutive fairs where I was doing up to 3 shows a day. It was insane, and my vocal chords felt like they were going through a cheese grater by the end of the summer.

Having pretty much lost my voice, I was desperate for help. I reached out to Renee Grant-Williams in Nashville. Everyone said she was the best, and they were right. When I told her I was losing my voice and experiencing pain, she said, " No problem, I can cure you of that in a few sessions." I was dubious that she could help me. She came across as really cavalier about the seriousness of my problem, and the worst part... she charged five-hundred bucks a session which to me was a frigging mint! She also had an impressive resume filled with A-list clients who swore by her services. She had helped people like Garth Brooks, The Dixie Chicks, Celine Dion, Christina Aguilera, and the list goes on and on, and I was duly impressed.

I'm so glad I paid that money. It was the best 500 dollars per hour I have ever spent. Yes, I went back for more sessions, and would've gladly shelled out the dough again if I ever had another problem. I learned that when you take the time to educate yourself, the results are always exponentially higher. I found out that her cavalier attitude was attributable to an absolute level of self-confidence. She knew her stuff like no one I'd ever known up until that time. She told me what I was doing wrong, showed me how to fix it, and guess what? I did exactly as she instructed and do you know why? Because I paid for that knowledge. That's right, if someone had given me the exact same advice for free, it is highly doubtful that I would've tried it, but I paid dearly for that knowledge and there is no way I was going to see that money go wasted. In retrospect, she probably didn't charge enough because I would've paid anything for what she taught me, and I don't just mean how to sing better... I mean how to listen to my mentors and value what they have to say.

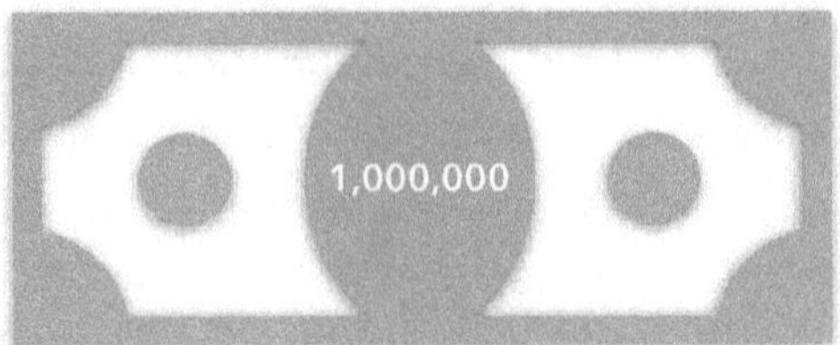

Later on in my career I had a good friend named Randy who was a financial planner, and I asked him for some advice one morning over coffee about maybe investing in some stocks and bonds. I'll never forget what he said... "No. I will not give you advice about that." I was taken aback. "Why wouldn't you help me, I thought we were friends?" I couldn't believe it. He said, "Look Doc, you're my friend and I'd do anything to help you, but I simply don't give advice to people who aren't paying me for it. It's not because I'm being stingy here, it's just that I have a lot of respect for the value of what I have to offer, and frankly, I've found that if I give that information away, it will be ignored. I care about you too much to do that to you. I want you to be successful financially, so I won't give you advice that I know you're not going to use, if you want to become a client, we'll talk."

I won't lie to you, I thought he was a jerk at the time, and I really didn't get it till years later when it happened to me. I had a good 50 students enrolled in my school and was doing extremely well for several years. I had pretty much all the work I could handle and was loving it. I was approached by a parent of a child at one of our rock and roll recitals in a local club one evening. She told me her kid was really quite talented and had a guitar and was already doing amazing things with it, but he really needed lessons and wanted to be a part of my recital system which would give him regular stage-experience. The only problem was, she just couldn't afford the tuition. Well, I didn't even think twice about it. I said, let me meet your child, if he's as talented as you say he is, I'll take him "pro bono." Like I said, I was doing well and wanted to give back so I signed this kid up for lessons. It was one of the biggest mistakes I've ever made.

I taught this kid for about three months and it pretty much went like this... First lesson, he was ten minutes late which threw every kid after him the rest of the day ten minutes late. This kid never did any of his assignments, he lost every handout I ever gave him, and hardly ever practiced. He did show up for recital night expecting to get a spot on stage, but that was it. Since he wasn't really doing what I was trying to teach him, I was reluctant to take credit for the mess he was making of the music. After three months of "free" lessons, this family "no showed" on fifty percent of his lessons, and was late by five to twenty minutes on the other fifty percent. He was the worst student I ever had, and one of only a few I've ever had to fire. They simply had no respect for my time or for that matter, the time of the other students in my school. After I expelled them, the family would continue to show up to my recitals and ask to get up with the band, but they would go around and say ugly things about me to the other parents. I had really and truly tried to do a nice thing for this family, and it ended up costing me again and again. It was an unfortunate situation. You tend to learn there most from the lessons that cost you money.

The only difference between this kid and every other kid I ever taught had been the fact that the family had paid nothing for his lessons. You may be thinking that kid and that family were awful and ungrateful, and maybe you're right, but maybe not. You see, I take full responsibility for what happened, and if that family were in this room today, I would give them my most sincere apologies for what I did to that kid. He may have been a great musician if not for my misguided attempt to teach him. You see, in giving away my services, I demonstrated to the family that I did not value what I was teaching, and if I didn't value it, why should they? The student-teacher relationship is a professional one, and I had made it unprofessional. That kid might've been great, but we'll never know because I cheapened the value of proper instruction. I did him and the family a disservice.

Now am I saying don't ever help anyone unless they pay you first? Not exactly. There will be people whom you mentor simply for the joy of that relationship, and there will be a few special ones that you mentor because they truly care about you and respect what you have to teach them. That is a relationship that takes years to build. But, there is an old saying that I believe bears repeating here... "Don't cast your pearls before swine." Be careful who you choose to "give" your pearls to, because it is a truly ugly feeling to see your best advice grossly disregarded or tossed aside as if it had no value. You have worked very hard, bleeding and sweating for all of the knowledge and experience you possess. Value it, or no one else will.

*Value your experience, or
no one else will*

Another key point I need to make here is this: Be a life-long learner. There will be song-writing workshops, production courses, creativity classes that come along. There is a world full of knowledge that will continue to make you better at everything you do. Some of it is free, available at the public library, some is not. You must take charge of your own professional development as a songwriter. No one is going to do it for you. You have got to continue to grow and develop yourself. This is just what professionals do. In the world of medicine and education, we are required to submit to continuing education in order to maintain our professional licenses. What are you doing on a regular basis to make yourself better at what you do? Know what your strengths and weaknesses are and seek the knowledge that will shore up your intellectual deficits and make you a stronger creator. That may mean investing in a university course in creative writing. It may mean investing in an online course or joining a professional writing organization. It may be reading this book. Whatever your goals, seek to better yourself constantly and be prepared to pay for that education. If you value yourself, invest in yourself. When you invest in that knowledge, you will be far more likely to act upon it.

"Genius without education is like
silver in the mine."
-Benjamin Franklin

Secret #22

Enjoy The Grind

If you cannot be happy everyday doing what you do, then you really shouldn't be doing it. Now there will always be certain mundane tasks that just aren't your favorite. These chores are unavoidable... taking out the trash, washing your car, etc. Whatever that thing is that you really don't care for.   That thing that you put off doing, groan when its unavoidable and eventually complain your way through.   In the end, you end up doing them anyway. You just took a crappy job and made it ten times worse by griping about it. I like to differentiate between *jobs* and *work*. To me, jobs are the things we have to do, work is the larger thing that all the jobs are part of. It is the job that is mundane, but work... work is the thing that we take pride in. We refer to a job in a generic way, but we take ownership of our work. For instance, you might say, "I have to do *a* job." But you would say this is part of *my* work." It is the jobs that make our work possible. The job is the thing we *have* to do, the work is the thing we *want* to do. It is the thing we *must* do in order to be the very best versions of ourselves. Never let your job get in the way of your work.

> Never let the job get in
> the way of the work

Most people rush through life from deadline to deadline. It's as if we are all racing to the end of something. Have you ever had someone "spoil" a movie ending for you? Did it enhance your pleasure when you saw it, or were you disappointed the whole time? Not long ago I overheard someone talking about a movie that I really wanted to see, so I sort of "tuned in" when they were talking about it behind me at the grocery store. Before I could tune back out, they had spilled the ending to *The Avengers Infinity War*. Suddenly, a movie I had greatly anticipated for over a year was a pending disappointment. I dreaded seeing it, even though I knew I would be dragged there by my son regardless of my prior knowledge. What's more, I would have to keep the secret safe from him which sullied the experience to an even greater extent.

I don't think I ever even told him that the ending had already been spoiled for me because I didn't want to lessen his experience in the least, and I knew it would. The point is, the movie hadn't changed, it was still the same spectacle that it would've been regardless, but somehow having prior knowledge of the ending just ruined the whole thing. Just like that, a billion dollars down the tubes, at least for me.... The lesson here is this, by skipping to the ending, we cheapen the entire experience. The ending is nothing without the beginning and the middle. Do you pick up a book and flip to the last chapter? No, you read the whole thing from the beginning. Do you skip to the chorus of the song? No, the chorus is great, but it is incomplete without the build-up that gets you there.

So why do we all race to the ending? Because the culture of America is hyper focused on the ending. We are so focused on the diploma that we fail to value the education it takes to earn it.   I went back to graduate school as an adult, and I was absolutely appalled to find fellow students, adults in their mid-twenties, people who were supposed to be becoming responsible medical professionals upon graduation… actually cheating on tests, quizzes and research papers. Why? I was there to learn, but I couldn't believe that some of the other students were only there for a diploma. Don't get me wrong, most of them were good students, but the cheaters were definitely present. So don't be so focused on the medal that you forget to take part in the race. Don't be so focused on the applause that you forget to enjoy the performance.

Goals are fine, they are necessary even, but they are not paramount to success. There are other more important factors that you must not fail to take into account.   A goal is merely *one* of many tools at your disposal. Do not become so focused on the goals that you forget to enjoy the moments that make up your life. We are a *goal* oriented society, and you can still be a goal oriented person, just don't become goal "disoriented."

I know right now I sound like the opposite of every self-help success manual you have ever read, but I'm not here to teach you just how to be successful in business or life. I'm trying to teach you how to be more creative, and a hyper-focus on goals alone will stymie your creativity. A person who is always looking ahead, reaching for the end will miss out on the beauty of the now.

Many of us go through our lives thinking, if I can just achieve this next thing I will be happy.   So you work your living butt off till you get it. Then after you get that thing you realize that it didn't make you happy at all, instead you are disappointed when by all accounts, you should be happy. Then you think, what the hell just happened? My life isn't about what I thought it was about. I'm not happy when I should be, and I don't know why.

These are the kinds of dilemmas that extraordinarily talented, goal oriented people struggle with all the time. Ever wonder how someone as successful and talented as Marilyn Monroe, Janis Joplin, Jimi Hendrix, Chris Cornell, Anthony Bourdain, and Robin Williams would kill themselves? I don't want to focus on the morose here, but the list goes on and on and on. I don't pretend to know what these amazing people were going through and it is not my intent to judge them for the decisions they made or didn't make that may have contributed to their untimely deaths. All I am saying is that achievement is not the key to happiness.   The people at the top, for better or for worse will eventually come to this conclusion, and they will either be happy in that realization, or they will become deeply depressed and may even be destroyed by it.

I don't know exactly why people become depressed at the top, and I wouldn't presume to trivialize the pain of these individuals in any way. However, I believe that it is important to try and understand the relationship between success and depression. I don't claim to have all the answers here by any means, but I do have a theory and I'm going to break it down for you. So this is, strictly speaking, my anecdotal theory of the success/depression relationship and not necessarily based on an investigation of the literature.

First, you lie to yourself and say, "this *achievement* will make me happy," you believe the lie, set a goal and focus on that one achievement with absolute determination and single mindedness until you have attained it. Once you have achieved it, you feel the inevitable "crash" that comes with the realization that this achievement didn't bring you happiness. Then the voice says, "now what?" So you set a new goal because you think, "maybe if I do something even more amazing I'll get that happiness I wanted." and the cycle begins again. You never actually get to enjoy the happiness that you *think* the achievement of the goal will bring you. There is no amount of fame or achievement that will make you happy. If you are only focused on the goal, then the opposite is true. The greater your achievement, the greater the disappointment after the goal is achieved. Eventually and inevitably it is despair which results. This can be an extremely painful process. Some of the most depressing times of my life have directly followed the greatest achievements of my life. It seems so very backwards and confusing, but it's true. So focus on what you are doing *right now*, and enjoy it to the fullest. The mountaintops are great, but they do not define you as an artist… that is the job of the work.

> True happiness is the job of
> the work

No, I don't believe in genius. I believe in freedom. I think anyone can do it. Anyone can be like Rembrandt.

-Damien Hirst

Secret #23

Never Hold Back

Always put your best foot forward. Always open with your best song, always lead with your best line. I don't know how many ways this can be said. Never hold back your best because you may not get another chance to show it. Oh what a tragedy it is to look back and say *I wish I would have done that other song first. I wish I had really shown them what I can do. I wish I would've brought out my best idea in that songwriting session.* To be told , "you're just not quite there yet, we're gonna pass." What are you going to say? *"Oh, I was sand bagging, I was just wasting your time, I can actually do a lot better."* By even thinking this way, you prove that you are not ready for whatever the opportunity is. What are you holding back for? There's never been a better time than right now. The past is full of regrets, the future is an illusion. *Now* is the only time that truly exists.

There is a saying that has been drilled into our heads so much that I only have to say part of it and you can finish it for me. Save the best for ______. Did you just say what I think you said? Were you able to fill in the missing word? Well, I hereby challenge the conventions of society and show business and I say this adage is a hindrance in most situations. I say don't save the best for last. You save your best for *first*.

I was honored to have been a guest on the Charlie Chase show once in Nashville, my plan was to start the show with a strong song, do a ballad after the sofa segment, you know where you sit and talk with the host, and then close the show with my strongest song. The one song I really wanted Nashville to hear on TV, the song that would've propelled me to International stardom sadly, never got played that day because I was bumped by another guest who went long. I made a big mistake and I learned this valuable lesson. This is the lesson that every writer should know and I should've known better. Never bury your lead. Never save your best for last. What if your first is your last? You just screwed yourself. Perform as if you might get bumped. In retrospect, I was a terrible guest, I probably got bumped on purpose… perhaps because I held back…. Food for thought.

When I was a young songwriter, wandering the streets of Nashville searching for my pot of gold, I would go into meetings all the time looking for someone to work with and they would always say something similar, "play me your best song." No one wanted to hear my second best song. And more often than not, if you are in some guy's office during business hours, you're lucky to even be there taking up his time. Be grateful to even get to play one song in a meeting because more often than not, you will not get the opportunity to play two. As you approach young middle age, like the author (you know… me), you begin to discern through the veil of success, all of the little failures the road is actually littered with… they are quite numerous actually, and painful to behold, *cringeworthy* one might even say. Not only is it difficult to look at your own failures, it is hard to see others make the same mistakes. You just want to take a young person and rap them on the head and say… "you're creating chaos right now, you're going to regret this for the rest of your life." But alas, I wish you all the joy of your awful and numerous mistakes. Allow me to explain…

I would like to honestly say that I am the best teacher you will ever have, but sadly that title goes to another much more worthy if not devilish maestro known as *experience*. It is not my intention to stop you from making all the mistakes that you are going to make. After all, if I did that effectively, I would be taking away from you the best teacher you will ever have. The worst mistakes teach the very best lessons in the most effective way possible, through experience. No, my purpose is not to stop you, my purpose here is to stop you from wasting years and years producing at a snails pace. My purpose is to accelerate your creative processes beyond your wildest dreams. *"But what if I make mistakes?"* You ask… My purpose is to get you to make lots and lots of mistakes as fast as you can and make them every single day of your life. If you are not making mistakes, you are not *doing* anything… You see, some people see mistakes as a bad thing, but mistakes are actually a badge of honor that remind you that you are indeed trying, that you efforts are being directed toward a worthwhile objective.

Haven't you been listening? If you are to truly live, you must be learning, and if you are to truly learn, you must be taking chances, and if you are truly taking chances, you will make mistakes, and if you are making mistakes, you are becoming a better person, and if you are becoming a better person, you are truly living. This is the real "circle" of life. We are all creators, and when you understand the creative process you really begin to understand this: you are the creative genius behind the masterpiece that is your life. I highly recommend that you live your life as if every day is an adventure, because it *can* be if you let it be. And when you make the mistakes, and you will… revel in them, because they are making you the person you truly want to become.

Your mistakes are your partners in growth, elevating you from ignorance to experience. When you make a big one, smile and tell the universe, "thank you." Learn and move on.

Avoid mistakes? nonsense! I say enjoy your mistakes. You made them, you may as well get something positive out of them. No one likes to be disappointed, but we all suffer failures along the way and if you are tiptoeing through life hoping to never make a mistake then the chances are, you are not doing anything worthwhile. You are not living a life worth remembering. Once you accept that you *are* going to make mistakes no matter how hard you try not to, it's liberating in a way. Accept the fact that you are going to screw up and royally. Then, expect to screw up every now and then. Don't misunderstand, I am not saying to be a negative influence on yourself, don't be a doom-seeker, you know, the type who go around predicting the end of the world constantly, the people who can't help but pop every balloon at the party. The people who have to find the dark cloud behind every silver lining. That is most definitely not what I'm talking about here.

All I am saying is that mistakes are inevitable. If you expect your train to jump the tracks every so often, you don't have to completely lose your shit every time it happens. When you screw up you can just point and say, oh there it is, now we should be good for awhile. You can look at the situation and ask yourself the question, "What am I supposed to learn here?" If there is a lesson, learn it and be thankful for it, if there's no lesson, which is rare, then just fix the problem and move on. Never waste the time *worrying* about a problem that could be better used to *solve* it.

Never waste time worrying

When I was young and dumb and full of misguided concepts about the world and how creativity works, I lived as I discussed earlier, in a world where ideas were few and far between. I would often be writing a song and come up with a line so good that I would say, well I better save that one and write a whole other song with that hook. It's too good to use in just another line…. Boy was I a dope. That was back when I wrote as if every idea were going to be my last, like most of the professional writers I knew. When you are writing and you decide to "hold back" a line or a phrase or an idea for later, it is like watering down your own liquor. No one likes to feel like their getting ripped off at the bar, no one likes to open a sack of chips and find out that they just bought a bag of air, and no one likes the feeling of being bamboozled, taken, grifted. So why, oh why would you do it to yourself? I will repeat myself once again for emphasis…. Never, ever hold back your very best. Especially not from yourself. When you are writing a song or a book or a sonnet, whatever you are creating, your ideas are coming fast and strong and they are coming to assist the process that is happening in the present. Concentrate all of your energy on what is happening *right now*. Don't save anything for the next song, because your creativity will still be there and stronger than ever when the next song comes. Ideas are like pebbles in the ocean, and the more you have, the more you will have. Imagine them in the abundance in which they truly exist. Touch your heart and say this with me out loud…

Genius hits a target no one else can see.

—Arthur Schopenhauer

Secret # 24

Be Grateful

While there are a multitude of strategies and tools at the disposal of the creative genius, gratitude is the glue that binds them all together. Every moment and every thing is a gift. As you reach for the coffee cup, how can you take for granted the gift of the beverage, the inspiring slogan printed on the front or the technology it took to manufacture and deliver it to your desk. What about the hand that prepared it? Was it your own? Then why not be thankful that you have the knowledge to prepare it, what about the skills it took to earn the money that purchased the beans, what about the hand that picked the beans in some far away land, and the hand that roasted those beans to perfection. Our lives are filled with examples. Look around the room you are sitting in. Identify one object and try to imagine every aspect of the journey it took that object to sit before you now and the value it added to the lives of people at every stage of the journey. I'm looking at a vocal microphone in absolute wonder as I write these words. I am every bit as awed by the skills and technology that it took to develop such a product as I am by the journey it took to arrive here in my life.

I can choose to make up a song today, sing it into that microphone and create an Mp4 file that others will want to own, collect, or synch with a video or audio file, thereby adding value to the world around me. That song that I create might be the spark some other person needed in order to create another product, it may enhance a television commercial which helps market another product which changes and adds value to other lives and so on forever into eternity. Every miracle that it took to bring that microphone to my desk makes the miracle of my own creativity possible, and thereby makes possible all of the future creativity it may help inspire. And on and on it goes. I am so grateful for my home, my family, my friends, my life, my health, and my skills. I believe that it is important to stop for a moment each day and truly appreciate every detail. There is something about the process of appreciation that is truly exhilarating. I look at a blank screen or an empty page and I see possibility. I see words taking shape, forming sentences, paragraphs or the lines of a song. I imagine page after page filling with arrangements of words with the power and intent to change lives and add incomprehensible and immeasurable value to those people. Every thought you think sends a ripple through your world, and every action you take can send ripples through the lives of countless others. That is the gift of the creative genius, and it is nothing short of magical.

Everyday I look at my life and my world and I try to truly appreciate what I have. I have a gratitude list in my cell phone, and anytime I feel the urge to complain or feel sorry for myself, I pull out that list and go through it. I say to myself, "I am so very thankful for…" and I go through that list. It is impossible to accomplish anything while you are feeling sorry for yourself or complaining about your lot in life. And it is impossible to feel sorry for yourself or complain while you are truly admiring all of the wonderful things you already have.

I consider the act of *complaining* a vice like smoking cigarettes because it is only satisfying to the person doing it, it's self destructive, and it poisons and/or annoys everyone else in the vicinity. Have you ever listened to someone complaining endlessly about something you didn't care about? Few conversations in life are quite so boring. You immediately want to get away from that situation, but it's so hard to extract yourself, so you nod your head and pretend to listen when all you really want to do is run. Remember that feeling the next time you are tempted to engage in it. You cannot create and complain at the same time… it is absolutely impossible.

To the creative genius, to indulge in this vice is a waste of time and energy. Choose instead to make the conscious decision to be thankful for everything you already have, your life will be richer for it, and your inner creative genius will thank you.   I encourage you to make the commitment to be thankful every single day. A lifestyle of gratitude will help boost your creativity to unprecedented heights. Touch your heart and say it with me.

> I will take a moment to be thankful every day for the rest of my life

The secret of genius is to carry the spirit of the child into old age, which means never losing your enthusiasm.

–Aldous Huxley

25

A Day In the Life

As you may have guessed by now, my whole life I've been an avid reader and consumer of the self-help category of books. Some of my favorites have been the ones that taught me how to do something that I didn't formerly know. I was always looking for a book that would change something about my life for the better. I suppose you could say I've spent a lifetime in search of any knowledge that might further my intellect or pave the way to greater success. My least favorite books are the ones that promised to teach me something useful and failed to deliver. My favorite books are those that promised and delivered practical advice including things that I could actually *do* to better myself. What I have tried my best to deliver in this book are practical tools that anyone can use to further and enhance their creativity. Whenever possible, I have included aspects of successful creativity which are supported philosophically by the wisdom of those great thinkers that came before us. In addition, I have tried here to bolster the authority of these strategies by utilizing both scientific and anecdotal evidence whenever possible. That being said, this is not a scientific journal, it is a collection of tools and methods that have worked for me and many others over a lifetime of intense creativity and exceptional productivity. I am grateful for the opportunity to share my methods and it is my sincere hope that you glean enough practical guidance from this book to boost you into the creative stratosphere.

As previously promised, this final chapter will take the reader through some practical application and examples of how these principles might apply to everyday creativity. This chapter will not be for everybody. In fact, I've never seen this done before in print, so it's either a very original idea and it's GENIUS, or it's never been done for a reason because it's crap. You be the judge. If it helps you great, if it does not, no worries.

At six o'clock this morning my eyes spring open and I immediately close them, willing my brain to recall what happened in there over the past several hours of sleep.

"Come on brain," I tell myself. "Surely there is something useful you can give me to work on today." I go through the last dream I had before awakening. I am in a forest outside my childhood home and it is dark and rainy. I am looking for my wife who is lost. I lose interest and cast this thought aside as I take a step deeper into my night. Images and thoughts rush past my closed eyes and through my open mind as I consider the significance of each one and either file it away or move past. I dreamed I was flying at some point and really enjoyed that dream. I smile as I think of myself soaring far away over rooftops in the night. I have a bit of a sore throat and consider I may have especially weird dreams tonight because I might be coming down with a cold or something. I push past the flying dream and there is something right on the tip of my consciousness that I can't quite seem to reach. I take a deep breath and try to clear my mind rather than reaching for the thought or idea. I remind myself that reaching for a thought is like playing tag with a fast runner. The closer you get the more it seems to barely escape your grasp. I relax and clear my wandering mind again and the thought comes into focus. I immediately reach for my cell phone to write it down.

"Miss you now" It's just a title, but the idea begins to form in my head and I know immediately it will be the start of a good song. I roughly sketch the idea as follows - "The singer knows that his lover will be leaving and he won't see her for a long while, so he vows to start missing her *now*. He anticipates being lonely and heartbroken without her around and wants her to understand his feelings."

I am tempted to keep writing on this idea, massaging it until it sounds like a hit song, but I resist the temptation and continue my meditation, mining even deeper into the previous night. I know this idea is a good seed and will be there when it is time to write later. I spend a few more minutes thinking about my dreams, but nothing else very useful seems to emerge, so I sit up in bed, close my eyes and continue my meditation, clearing my mind again. This time I think of my childhood, conjuring a clear picture of the trailer I grew up in. I picture the dilapidated green shutters, the sheet metal door and the cheap aluminum screen. I go inside and see the worn out linoleum floor and the filthy carpet. I see the thick layer of cigarette smoke hanging as the sunlight beams through the windows, illuminating the dusty air. I feel the pain of that poverty, the humiliation of going to school without proper shoes, walking to the bus stop in the cold without a coat in the winter and the shame of being ridiculed by the other children and even my teacher at school. I fast forward to the present and see and feel and appreciate how happy and prosperous my life is. I think of how grateful I am for my beautiful home, my lovely wife, my happy children and my awesome car. A wave of gratitude goes through me body like chills. Next I fast forward to the future and imagine an even better life. I imagine how awesome it would be to be even happier. I imagine what my world will look like in ten years. I imagine my new vacation condo in downtown Nashville in great detail. I visualize the list price of seven hundred thousand and shrug my shoulders... *no hill for a climber* I think to myself. I imagine the numbers in my brokerage account. I imagine how many shares of Netflix I want to own. I think of what car I want next. I see materialized, a new Tesla Roadster Coupe in my garage and see my wife getting in it to go to the grocery store. *Get your own dream car!* I call out to her with a smile. I imagine the life I want and I literally feel the joy of already having all of my dreams come true.

I clear my mind and spend the next several minutes straining to think of absolutely nothing but my own breathing…

The alarm goes off and I hop out of bed and spend the next 15 minutes doing all my necessaries. I brush my teeth, forcing myself to use my left hand and force my mind to focus on the experience of the present. The feel of the toothbrush, the tone of the hum, the tingling of the toothpaste against my gums. I focus all of my energy and thoughts on each individual tooth as I clean them one by one. My mind tries to trail off, but I bring it back each time. I place the toothbrush back down and move on to the next and the next and the next task, thinking my way through each one in turn until I am dressed and ready.

Next, I walk into the kitchen where my wife has a cup of coffee ready for me already. I kiss her and then turn to add the usual ingredients to my cup. A tablespoon of MCT oil this morning should do the trick along with a scoop of collagen peptides powder. As I sip my coffee, I prepare six eggs and sit down and visit with my wife for a few minutes. When breakfast is done I head into my office, limit distractions and begin writing. I take the new idea from my dream last night and begin brainstorming, shooting for as many ways as possible to spin the idea into a fresh hook. After producing a full page of possibilities, I decide to let that idea sit for the time being and instead turn to my piano and start playing around with a melody that's swimming around in my head. I immediately touch onto something pretty and grab my cell phone and lay down a voice memo of the idea.

There is a song that I've been working on for a few months for a musical I am working on called "Sydistic." I've been trying to spend a bit of time on it daily. I call this particular song a *slow burn* because it seems to be inching along bit by bit over an excruciatingly slow period of time. The musical genre is a bit unfamiliar to me, so that may be the reason for the delay in production. I've already finished three songs for this musical and written a good portion of act one of the script, but I anticipate this is going to take me a year to complete so there's no hurry. I go back to my computer and pull up my Google Keep folder and begin going through the lyrics that are already written there. I pick out one and sing it to myself over and over, trying new melodies and playing around with the chords until the right one materializes. The time flies by as I concentrate through the writing session and soon two hours have passed. I move on to the next phase of my day.

It's time for me to go to my day job. As a child I always wanted to be a medical professional and so I returned to school as an adult and trained to be a therapist and still practice in the field of home health. It suits me because there is no set schedule, it takes me to many homes and patients and I need all that visual, intellectual and auditory input to stimulate new ideas which I constantly jot down throughout the day. At the end of my work day, I might return to my studio with a dozen or more ideas for new songs. I have a voice to text option on my phone and a note pad on my car's computer screen where I can jot down ideas as they come, and I can always pull over for a few minutes and write something if I need to.

At lunch time I pull into a convenience store and grab an unsweetened iced tea. As I stand in line, I smile at the lady in the line next to me. She is haggard and does not appear to be friendly in the least, but when she sees me smile she lifts her eyebrows and returns it as best she can. I start thinking about a *half-hearted smile* and begin turning the phrase over and over in my mind, trying to mold it into a hook, but nothing much happens there. I pull out my cell phone and jot the idea down in my folder, pay for my drink and head out to my car. I realize that even though a hook didn't jump out at me immediately, the idea goes into the file anyway because it may jump out at me a year down the road. You just never know. When I get out to my car I realize that I'm feeling a little tired so I close my eyes and clear my mind for a few minutes, allowing my brain to rest. After a few minutes have passed, I head to my next patient and the day continues.

After all the patients have been seen I head back home, let the dog out of the house, play with her awhile, then return to the studio where I finish up my *work*-work for the day, documenting all the patient's I saw and making sure all my work emails have been cleared. When all my jobs have been completed for the day, I return to my work in the studio. It is now four thirty in the afternoon and I have a good hour left before my wife gets home, at which time I will peel myself out of the studio and go hang out with her for awhile and have dinner. We will probably watch a little TV, visit with my children and just hang out. Of course, she doesn't mind that I have my phone handy in case an idea strikes or someone says something clever that I have to write down, but at this point in the day, I'm done working so there's no pressure.

I get ready for bed, I pull out my phone, plug it in, turn off the ringer and open my Google Keep folder. I pick a song that I'm stuck on and think of it as I turn off the light. As I am going to sleep, I clear my mind and think only of that song. I literally tell my brain that we are going to work on this song tonight. Please have it ready in the morning when I wake up. I smile and drift off to sleep. Maybe my brain will obey, maybe it won't… but every so often, it does. Perhaps genius is simply the ability to take the chaos and the mundane and bend it to your will daily. Creation is a miracle that occurs every day right under you nose and the creative genius is no more than an astute observer lurking at every turn. You can reap its benefits if you will only pay attention.

Perhaps genius is simply the ability to take the chaotic and the mundane and bend it to your will daily.

-<u>Doc Bates</u>

26

Wrapping It Up

Curiously, when I set out to write this book, I thought the hardest part would be coming up with stuff to write about. As it happens, the hardest part has been when to shut up and declare it finished. For the perfectionist, coming to a stopping point in one's work can be quite a challenge. Believe me when I say, the irony of this chapter is not lost on me. But the struggle, being quite real and daunting has led to much reflection upon whether or not to include a chapter on "wrapping up." To the creative genius, the process of creation involves many hours of revision and editing to perfect the work. But that perfection comes at a high cost. At some point we all have to let go of a project and let it be, for better or worse, what it will be.

If you find yourself stuck endlessly repeating the editing process over and over, you have several options. You can: get help, move on, release the work, or just start over. Throughout this book I have offered many strategies and how to boost and enhance creativity, but if all of your projects are getting stalled at the end, what have you accomplished? While I don't have all the answers, and some may not apply well to your individual situation, as a writer, I have come up with a few strategies that seem to work well for both myself and other writers I know.

Getting Help

Present your work to an individual or to a panel of friends. There are many Facebook groups devoted to this very purpose. Personally, I prefer to share directly with people whom I trust and respect. If you are going to seek and employ advice from others, it really needs to be from people whom you believe are creating at or above your current level. If you are a writer, there are many groups you can get involved and meet with personally. If you are a songwriter, you likely have a local NSAI (Nashville Songwriters Association International) chapter who meets monthly. But whether you are a painter, baker, or writer, or some other creative genius, there is a group for you out there. Find them and bounce your ideas off of them. Let your peers help to tell you when your work is ready.

Moving On

I have to admit that, while I write a staggering volume of songs and essays and jokes and anecdotes, not all of them come to rest on the minds and hearts of others. Some of that work product does not make it out of my studio. Taking Prince as an example, he died with thousands upon thousands of songs that were never released. Some would say that they were not truly "finished" because they were not recorded to a standard of finality one would find on a record. Likewise, you may find yourself having to move on to the next project from time to time just to keep the work flowing. If Prince would've stopped after every song was written and took the thirty or forty hours per song that it took to truly "finish" the material and record it, he would've died with far fewer songs in his vault. Admittedly I'm just spitballing here, but I imagine that most of his backlog of material consisted of quite abbreviated and simple arrangements which were recorded with just a few instruments. And I'm sure that for the most part, it was brilliant work. That being said… even Prince knew when to move on to the next song, and so should we. Personally, I believe that moving on can be one of the greatest strategies you possess. Often when I employ this strategy, I add it to my circle back list and revisit it at a later date.

Release The Work

Sometimes the best judge of the quality of the work is the market. You can endlessly poke and nitpick on your work forever, but you will ultimately never know its true value until you discover what the market is willing to pay for it. Recording artists seldom release a full album these days before testing the market with a few singles. Often, a single is released before the album has even finished production. Record labels are in the business of making money from intellectual property. Take this lesson to heart and learn it well. They know what they are doing. So if you are unsure of the value of your work… release it and you will get your answer soon enough.

Start Over

Some would say that releasing one's work is the hardest thing an artist can do, but I beg to differ. Starting over from scratch is far more difficult. I have a friend whom I love and respect greatly. She has been of immense encouragement to me over the past several years. I was in her studio one day looking at her paintings and I stopped at one, puzzled, and tilted my head. She said bluntly, "It doesn't look like my work." I couldn't put my finger on why… but she was right. All of the ingredients were there. The colors, the textures, it was all present, but something was just missing and for a moment it drove me crazy trying to figure it out. I mean, it was still a beautiful painting, her time and materials invested in it were worth thousands of dollars, but her words were undeniable... it didn't look like her work. What bravery, to be able to look at one's work and acknowledge this simple truth.   I have often been astonished at her absolute mastery, but in this instance, I was even more astonished at her willingness to let go. I said to her, "What do you do with the one's that aren't quite right?" She pointed to the lake. "I commit them to the deep." There is no vault where her "almost" perfect paintings lie waiting to be rediscovered, touched up and sold. Her word choice, "commit" is descriptive and absolute.

What a wonderful lesson she taught me. To the creative genius, there is a time to just start over. There's only so much you can do to try and salvage a project, some of them will wind up at the bottom of the lake. If you recognize this eventuality, it won't come as quite a shock when it happens to you.   I like to think that there is some ceremony to the process. Words are said... the painting is released and goodbyes are wept as it slowly drifts away and out of sight and into the waves. Maybe those "words" are curses... Who knows? I didn't ask. I just hope you have the courage to do the same when the time comes, and the wisdom to know when the time comes.

Have the courage to commit your failures to the deep and start over.

-Doc Bates

27

Daily affirmations

<u>Sunday</u>

I am a creative genius

I am incapable of quitting

I was born to teach someone else what I
know

My ideas are as abundant as pebbles in an
ocean

I will take a moment to be thankful every
day for the rest of my life

<u>Monday</u>

I am a creative genius

The Blank Page Is My Friend

I take full responsibility for my own
creativity or lack thereof

There is no amount of natural talent that I
cannot out work

<u>Tuesday</u>

I am a creative genius

I create my own scarcity or abundance

My every idea has ten more behind it pushing
it out

I owe it to myself and my loved ones to do
what makes me happy

<u>Wednesday</u>

I am a creative genius

I will work to develop the skills necessary to succeed

I am the author of my own story

I must work as if I have no talent

<u>Thursday</u>

I am a creative genius

I rule my thoughts they do not rule me

I will conquer Mr negative

I will visualize success daily

<u>Friday</u>

I am a creative genius

I choose to become the master of my own thoughts

I will never let an idea get away

I will eat like a success

<u>Saturday</u>

I am a creative genius

I will seek co-writing experience and learn

My brain creates for me twenty-four hours

I will create and maintain a healthy work balance in my life

Print these affirmations out and hang them somewhere you will see them every morning and remember to say them out loud. This is an important strategy that will help train your brain to focus on maximizing your creativity.

Please visit

www.docbates.com

For free downloads, creative content and join the creative collective for exclusive updates and opportunities to springboard your creativity into the stratosphere. Thank you so much for making this book a part of your journey. It is my most sincere wish that you will make all of your dreams come true.

About the Author

Doc Bates is a recording artist, writer, composer, teacher, entrepreneur, entertainer, therapist, and lecturer with over 35 years of experience. He spent his early career in sales, moved into the music business full-time in 1995 and spent the next 10 years on the road with his band, touring, recording and entertaining before millions of fans. After being side-lined by a life-changing injury, Doc founded a Kansas City based school for young entertainers and began training others. Fifteen years later, alumni of Doc's school can be found all over the music industry as artists, producers, songwriters, teachers, and performers. Doc continues to write every day and instructs and mentors young artists and entertainers from his home in Lake Lotawana, Missouri where he lives with his wife, youngest son, and German shepherd, Scout. Doc writes on average, a song a day....

You can visit Doc at www.docbates.com or follow on facebook or instagram.

In memory of

Lawton Dawson Murray,

my greatest mentor

Just the beginning...